# THE VICTORY MOTORCYCLE

## THE MAKING OF A NEW AMERICAN MOTORCYCLE

MICHAEL DAPPER AND LEE KLANCHER

MBI Publishing Company

First published in 1998 by MBI Publishing Company, 729 Prospect Avenue, PO Box 1, Osceola, WI 54020-0001 USA.

MBI Publishing Company books are also available at discounts in bulk quantity for industrial or sales-promotional use. For details write to Special Sales Manager at MBI Publishing Company Wholesalers & Distributors, 729 Prospect Avenue, PO Box 1, Osceola, WI 54020-0001 USA.

Library of Congress Cataloging-in-Publication Data

Dapper, Michael
    Victory motorcycle: the making of a new american motorcycle/ Michael Dapper and Lee Klancher
        p. cm.
    Includes index.
    ISBN 0-7603-0530-7 (pbk. : alk. paper)
    1. Victory motorcycle. I. Klancher, Lee,
    II. Title.  III. Series.
TL448.V43D37        1998
629.227'5--dc21                    97-14857

Text by Michael Dapper
Photos and captions by Lee Klancher

Edited by Paul Johnson
Designed by Tom Heffron

Printed in Hong Kong through World Print, Ltd.

**On the front cover**

*A Victory preproduction bike from the CV series on November 12, 1997. The CV, or concept vehicle, bikes were the third generation of Victory-engined prototypes. The bike was photographed at the Polar Aviation Museum at Anoka County Airport in Blaine, Minnesota. The lovely plane in the background is a Hawker Sea Fury.* Lee Klancher

**On the frontispiece**

*The V92C was tested in a variety of conditions, including heavy near-freezing rain that was wiped to a blur in this shot.* Lee Klancher

**On the title page**

*Engineer Mario Negri and a CV bike cruise the canyons. Negri played a crucial role in refining the frame and, like much of the staff, put considerable time in test riding prototypes.* Lee Klancher

# CONTENTS

# ACKNOWLEDGMENTS

Sincere thanks for the cooperation, candor, patience, and time of all our sources, especially those members of the Victory team who sat for interviews during long workdays as the bike approached completion.

Special thanks to Victory team members, such as General Manager Matt Parks, Engineering Manager Geoff Burgess, Mark Bader, Steve Weinzerl, John Garms, Kevin Mollet, Gary Gray, Jeff Hugett, Mario Negri, Robin Tuluie, Todd Sigfrid, Mike Mills, Steve Paulos, and Jennifer Rud.

Gratitude also goes to Polaris personnel who lent assistance, including Snowmobile General Manager Bob Nygaard, Corporate Communications Manager Marlys Knutson, Nancy Krenz and Leanne Koivisto.

Motorbooks International staffers who made this possible include: President Tim Parker, Publishing Director Jack Savage, Editor Paul Johnson, Production Manager Jana Solberg, Print Buyer Sharon Gorka, and Designer Tom Heffron. Our thanks.

Others who offered support and deserve thanks include: Sonja and Grace Dapper, Wayne Davis, Jerry Hatfield, Henry Fiola, Max Allers, Thomas Teske, Gary Gilbertson, and Mitsu Bayless.

*Michael Dapper*

First and foremost, thanks to the folks at Victory. They took time to answer questions and dig up images when they were already working 14-hour days and made motorcycles available for photographs when the bikes needed to be elsewhere. It was a genuine pleasure to work with the Victory people; their cooperation and open-mindedness created an essentially uncut view of the creation of the V92C.

In addition to the Victory members mentioned by Mike Dapper, I'd like to thank Cory McWhorter, Scott Dieltz, Dave Muckenhern, Mike Benoy, Mike Danielson, Chuck Crone, Al Regelstad, Dewey Voss, Marshall Tennerman, Jay Schilling, Tom Neil and the rest of the Spirit Lake crew. A special thanks to Victory staffers Mark Bader, Steve Weinzerl, and Jennifer Rud, who made extra efforts to help me out.

Thanks are due to chase truck driver Mike Haenggi, fellow MBI staffer Bob Wilson, and the folks at Motorbooks for making this happen. Thanks to Dave Barley and all the guys at Polar Aviation.

Last but never least, thanks to my wife, Renee. She makes all of this worth doing.

*Lee Klancher*

# **INTRODUCTION**

So you've created an all-new, top-quality, high-performance cruiser motorcycle.

Congratulations. Now do it again.

That's right. Your reward is the challenge of creating a second one exactly like your original. Then produce 10 of them, then 100, 1,000, 5,000, and more, all within extremely tight tolerances so you can't tell Number 0002 from Number 4886.

Building a top-quality motorcycle is eminently possible; custom builders do it all the time. But mass-producing and successfully marketing such a motorcycle is a daunting challenge. Just ask the people who have tried to revive the Indian motorcycle. They got as far as displaying a mocked-up bike with a wooden engine at Sturgis several years ago, but no real motorcycle has emerged. It won't either, without facilities and staff to carry out tasks such as engineering, manufacturing, distribution, and sales. Did we say it was a "daunting challenge?" How about staggering, or near impossible?

As the first Victory V92C was trucked out of the Spirit Lake, Iowa, manufacturing facility, Victory became the first mass-produced, all-new brand of American motorcycles since the 1940s.

According to motorcycle historian and author Jerry H. Hatfield, "The last American motorcycle to enter production was Mustang. Mustang went on the market in 1945 and quit in 1965."

The Mustang was a Rodney Dangerfield of motorcycles, failing to earn universal respect because of its small (12-inch) wheels. Hatfield said, "Mustangs came with a three- or four-speed foot-shift transmission and a telescopic fork, and they had plenty of pep up to their top speed of 65–70 miles per hour. They also had a loud thump-thump exhaust note as good as anything else."

A Pasadena, California, firm built at least one prototype Vard motorcycle around 1946, but that bike never went into production. (Vard, however, subsequently produced aftermarket telescopic forks for Indians and Harley-Davidsons.)

Unlike Indian, Excelsior-Henderson, and ACE, Harley-Davidson is the lone American motorcycle manufacturer to have survived into the latter stages of this century. Today, Harley-Davidson holds about a 50-percent market share of the worldwide cruiser market. Its sales success in the past decade has revved up competition from

Japanese manufacturers, and while they try to build a better Harley-style bike to compete with the Milwaukee-based leader, it takes their combined sales numbers to challenge Harley-Davidson's market share.

With so few long-term American motorcycle success stories on record, what makes Polaris think it can successfully produce a motorcycle? Plenty, including its manufacturing history, engineering talent, business savvy, and loyal Polaris customers.

Polaris has produced recreational vehicles for over 44 years. It has the engineering talent and production capabilities to design and produce three (so far) distinctly different vehicle lines and produce its own engines for many of those vehicles.

Polaris has also had the corporate leadership, notably from Chief Executive Officer W. Hall Wendel Jr., to forge a successful, profitable path through the 1980s and 1990s. In 1981, Wendel led a group of investors who purchased Polaris Industries back from Textron, which in 1968 had bought the company from its original Roseau, Minnesota, ownership group.

*Polaris' motorsports heritage dates back to 1954, when the company produced its first snowmobile. Co-founder and former CEO Alan Hetteen guided the company to early prosperity by selling snowmobiles for utility and, later, recreation. Polaris Industries Inc.*

The company has grown and diversified with Wendel at the helm. With Victory, it diversifies further.

## Victory Continues the Diversification

Polaris had built a 30-year reputation as a leading snowmobile manufacturer before its first major diversification in 1985 when it began producing all-terrain vehicles (ATVs). Even though the ATV industry was shortly thereafter rocked by the federal government's ban on three-wheelers and tight restrictions on the manufacture of four-wheelers, Polaris persevered and has become a leader in the ATV business. ATV sales accounted for 45 percent of the company's $1 billion-plus sales revenue in 1997, putting ATV sales on a par with snowmobiles, which had produced 60 percent of the company's revenue as recently as 1991.

In 1992 Polaris successfully diversified further, introducing a personal watercraft (PWC). The watercraft division has matured and expanded, and the 1998 product line consists of five different models. While Polaris watercraft haven't yet captured as significant a market share as have the ATVs, Polaris is one of the top four PWC manufacturers in the world, and the PWC division generated 7 percent of the company's 1997 sales revenue.

The addition of the ATV product line coincided with the company's change in 1987 from a limited partnership to a publicly traded company. In the past decade, the ATVs and watercraft have made the Polaris name known well beyond the snowbelt. The diversification has also expanded the Polaris dealer network, which now stretches across North America and the world.

Since becoming a publicly traded company, Polaris has generated a terrific return to shareholders. Stock splits and lucrative dividends were the rule, not the exception, for several years after the initial stock offering. The company continues to consistently pay dividends each quarter, and in 1995 the company achieved sales of $1 billion for the first time, a feat it repeated in 1996 (along with a 7-percent increase) and, for a third consecutive year, in 1997.

With the addition of the ATV and Personal Watercraft divisions, Polaris showed it's not content to let its future hinge on only one—or two—product lines. Turn the clock back to the early 1990s: With the successful PWC introduction completed, Polaris continued to consider acquisitions or expansions into additional businesses. The question was asked within the company's Minneapolis, Minnesota, headquarters: "What next?"

# 1

# MARKET RESEARCH AND A GO-AHEAD
## Hula-Hoops, Golf Carts, and Motorcycles!

Have you read the bestseller *Mowers and Mulchers: The Polaris Story*? Does your bookshelf contain a hardcover copy of *Off-Road Riding in Sand Traps: The Polaris Golf Cart Story*? Well, if Polaris had appointed someone other than Matt Parks as general manager of new products, there's the chance this book would be a book about Victory golf carts or lawn mowers—not motorcycles.

Parks, now 34, grew up in California with a love of motorcycles. He also loved tinkering around with machinery, which led him to the California Polytechnic State University–San

*Polaris CEO W. Hall Wendel Jr. sits behind Al Unser Jr. at the Victory's introduction to the press held in Bloomington, Minnesota, on June 26, 1997. Wendel's leadership has diversified Polaris with tremendous success. This vision of branching out beyond snowmobiles made possible the bike's introduction at the Mall of America, which featured Little Al riding PD-5, an early preproduction bike, into the throng of press packed into Planet Hollywood restaurant. Wayne Davis*

Luis Obispo, which offers some excellent mechanical engineering courses—and handy access to countless miles of roads that are ripe for spectacular motorcycle rides. However, Parks entered the school's business program and graduated with a B.S. in business with a concentration in marketing, and joined Polaris in 1987 as the district sales manager for California, Nevada, and Arizona. Since the company had only recently introduced its ATVs, his territory had a fledgling dealer network, and the Polaris brand had low name recognition. Parks' charge was to develop the dealer network in the region, and he succeeded, showing enough promise and potential to be named ATV product manager in February 1992.

His knowledge, attitude, and ability to analyze businesses in which Polaris was involved impressed management. Once he was settled in the company's Minnesota headquarters, management—specifically, Chief Executive Officer

*The roots of the Polaris company reside in the snow. A dominant force in the snowmobile industry, Polaris has a fiercely loyal customer base that rivals Harley-Davidson in fanaticism. This is a 1998 Polaris Indy XLT. Polaris Industries Inc.*

W. Hall Wendel Jr.—sought his opinions and had him do research on prospective acquisitions or expansions.

"Starting early in 1993, for whatever reason, I would be called in and told, 'Take a look at the such-and-such market. Let's look at go-karts or golf carts or lawn-and-garden, chain saws or whatever,'" Parks recalled. "I would find out about the industry and who the players are, how big it is and whether it's being well-served, its new trends and whatnot, and I'd present these findings to Hall.

"But," he said, "nothing really came of it." At least not at first.

He eventually got a second title, that of general manager of new products, which led to some interesting mail.

"I was sent every Hula-Hoop and every Rube Goldberg device from every quack in the country," Parks said. "They'd say, 'This is a new product. We want you to put Polaris on the side and sell it for $19.95.' But we *did* get a lot of fun stuff out of it to test."

None of the prospective new ventures panned out or even called for extensive research—until the need arose for a study of the off-road motorcycle market.

"A couple of companies came up for sale in the dirt bike business, the off-road motorcycle business, and we took a look at that," he recalled. "We studied the dirt bike business intensely, then a motorcycle company came to visit us to see if there was an opportunity to distribute their European motorcycles through Polaris.

"That sparked a study of the motorcycle business that uncovered signs of a promising market. Along with the dirt bike research, we did a quick study of the street bike business at that time, and we were kind of interested. We thought, 'You know, this makes some sense.'"

*In 1985 Polaris took its first step beyond snowmobiles and entered the ATV market. The entrance proved highly successful, and Polaris has become a powerful force in the ATV industry. This 1998 Sportsman 500 is a sport-utility model powered by a four-valve, four-stroke, single-cylinder, 500-cc engine. Polaris Industries Inc.*

## Polaris Owners Show an Interest

Polaris inserted a survey form in a 1993 issue of the company's *Spirit* magazine, which at the time was mailed to more than 300,000 Polaris vehicle owners. The survey measured readers' interest in a wide variety of products, from fishing boats to lawn-and-garden equipment to on- and off-road motorcycles. Respondents were asked if they would be interested in buying such products from Polaris.

"Motorcycling did really, really well [in the survey]," Parks said, "so we said, 'Well, this looks interesting; let's take a look; let's get some outside input.' We wanted to see if there was some opportunity in motorcycling, to see if it was a match with Polaris."

Wendel appointed two product managers—Parks and Snowmobile Division General Manager Bob Nygaard—to conduct further confidential research on motorcycles. Parks

and Nygaard hired two outside firms to assist them in the project: the McKenzie Company, one of largest consulting firms in the world, and Minneapolis advertising executive Jerry Stahl, who was very familiar with recreational motorsports and the motorcycle business. (As an ad agency executive, Stahl had worked on Harley-Davidson advertising campaigns.)

Meanwhile, Parks and Nygaard assessed the Polaris "infrastructure," that is, the company's sales force, dealer network, service and warranty operation, and parts, garment, and accessories division.

"We also looked at our customers to see the types of things they were interested in and whether they would buy a motorcycle from us," Parks said. "We worked on that pretty hard from May until August [1993]—extremely hard—and the upstairs conference

*The next step for Polaris came in 1992, when the company offered its first personal watercraft. Watercraft also came to provide a significant portion of the Polaris financial pie. Powered by a 135-horsepower, three-cylinder, 779-cc, two-stroke engine, the SLX Pro 785 represents the top of the performance heap for Polaris watercraft in 1998. Polaris Industries Inc.*

*Matt Parks looked at everything from go-karts to chain saws as possible avenues for Polaris. When the results of a 1993 survey showed a high number of Polaris owners were also motorcyclists, Parks and company executives began to seriously consider adding a motorcycle to the Polaris line. Parks is shown at the June 1997 press introduction. Victory*

room [in the company's Minneapolis head-quarters] was turned into our war room. We had our stuff pinned all over the room."

Nygaard said the motorcycle research effort was different from those connected with the company's previous diversification projects.

"We had an outside consulting firm [for the Victory project], which we had never done before," Nygaard said. "We didn't do that when we got into ATVs or watercraft. We had high-powered outside consultants. We brought in Jerry Stahl and talked to him. The research was more sophisticated than we did in the past, and another thing is, with motorcycles you had good [sales] numbers. You had Motorcycle Industry Council [MIC] numbers; you could tell where they were selling; you could see displacement, types of bikes, that kind of thing. And with the watercraft business, nobody knew. We would ask, 'How many watercraft are being built?' Nobody knew."

The Victory research showed there were opportunities for another manufacturer in the cruiser business, particularly if a newcomer was able to fulfill unsatisfied consumer demand for product, features, and performance.

"We focused in on Harley and the Japanese manufacturers and said to ourselves, 'Is Harley vulnerable from any standpoint?' We thought that their costs were high," Nygaard said. "We thought that, based on re-engineering the Harley bike, we could build it for less money. We felt that customers were waiting too long to take delivery of their Harleys, and they [H-D] were vulnerable from that standpoint. We could get to market with a bike that we could make money on, and the heavy cruiser end of it was certainly what we wanted to target because that's where the [sales] numbers were, and that's where the [profit] margin was. It was the best fit for us, in that the Japanese were vulnerable there. They really hadn't been able to tackle Harley, because it might look like a Harley, but the real rider knew that it wasn't an American-made bike from an American manufacturer. We were close [at the time] to being in the domestic engine business, and we could build our own U.S. engine, and that gave us a major leg up on the Japanese. We were an American company."

While still serving as the ATV product manager, Parks traveled the country. He interviewed dealers and consumers, attended motorcycle events, and compiled data along with the McKenzie firm and Stahl. Parks and Nygaard provided the company's officers with monthly updates and presented their conclusions to the officers in August 1993.

## Believe It or Not: Yes

"The result of the study was, believe it or not, yes, there was a tremendous opportunity in the motorcycle market," Parks said. "It's not the off-road motorcycle market; it's the on-road motorcycle market, and the entry point, the best entry point, would be in the cruiser market. Effectively, there was an oligopoly in the motorcycle market. There were just a very few players selling to the motorcycle market, and in the cruiser business, the Japanese were getting stronger and stronger, and that entire business was growing, and it appeared there was decent money to be made there."

The manufacturing capabilities and technological know-how required to produce cruisers seemed within Polaris' grasp, Parks said.

"There were fairly long product life cycles, and the technology was manageable," he said. "In other words, we weren't making a moon shot here. The technology was certainly advanced, and there's good high-end engineering that goes into the product. But we didn't need a Cray supercomputer to do this kind of thing. It's not NASA."

The research confirmed an established trend among cruiser owners: A high percentage of cruiser buyers, especially Harley-Davidson customers, immediately replace a few, or even many, components on their brand-new motorcycles. The Polaris research showed that cruisers have tremendous appeal—due in great part to the image they bestow upon riders—even though their performance or component quality is sometimes subpar. Riders upgrade things such as brakes and intake systems for better performance, change seats for greater comfort, and install aftermarket exhausts to change the exhaust sound.

"The research showed there was some opportunity, it appeared, to do a better job, based on what customers were telling us and based on what the aftermarket said," Parks said. "We found it very interesting that, aside from the cosmetic features in the cruiser business, so many people change the functional attributes of their current motorcycles. Many of them [make changes] right away [to new bikes]. Why are they changing the wheels, the brakes, and the tires and stiffening the frames and adding vibration-absorption devices that

*Although Polaris considered building an off-road motorcycle, a closer look at the market led them to believe that the best opportunity existed in the cruiser market. Cruisers were becoming increasingly popular; customers were waiting several years for Harley-Davidsons, and the technology required to be competitive was attainable for a company starting from scratch.*

you don't even see? Why are they putting on aftermarket suspensions? Some of it is obviously cosmetic, but a lot of it was functional. We needed to understand that."

Perhaps Polaris *could* make a better cruiser, but did it make business sense? Remember, shareholders were used to successful new product ventures—and used to receiving quarterly dividends.

"In August 1993, we got the okay from our officer group to continue with the study," Parks said. "We all agreed that there is an opportunity in the street motorcycle business and in cruisers. We needed to determine if it fit into our manufacturing systems and whether we could make any money at it."

Nygaard said the Victory research team certainly recognized the risks of entering the cruiser market, especially considering the profitable popularity of the Harley-Davidson culture and the "Harley rider" image and style.

"My biggest concern was: Let me sell against price, let me sell against features and benefits, let me sell against more advertising, and I can find ways to do that," Nygaard said. "Help me to sell against the lifestyle, with loyalty that is as passionate as I've ever seen on any product [Harley-Davidson]. To sell against an image is very, very difficult, and that was my biggest concern."

## Make or Buy the Parts?

The Polaris team expected that the answer would be yes, they *could* make money in the motorcycle business, but they needed to determine what it would cost to build a cruiser. They did a "make versus buy" evaluation to determine which components they could produce in-house and which they would likely buy from outside vendors. In 1993 they bought a Honda Shadow and a Harley-Davidson FXRS, took them completely apart, estimated the cost of every single part, and determined for each part whether they would make it or buy it.

They factored in the suggested retail prices of the Honda and Harley, the dealer costs of the bikes, and the profit margin that would be required at various sales volumes.

"We came back, and we felt, 'Wow, there's good opportunity in this business!' So we were excited from that standpoint," Parks said. "The motorcycle would, as it turned out, fit very nicely into our existing systems, whether we built the bike in Roseau or wherever else."

But what about the engine? Polaris' market studies had shown that for greatest acceptance and sales appeal, a cruiser *must* have an American-made engine. Recall Nygaard's comment about the diminished acceptance of Japanese-made—that is, not American-made—bikes.

At the time, Polaris hadn't yet launched its domestic engine program (which today produces engines for its snowmobiles and personal watercraft), but it felt that finding a U.S. engine supplier would not be a significant stumbling block.

"Our assumption," Parks said, "was 'we can build this engine inside [Polaris] or at least have it built in the United States .'"

In February 1994, Parks and then-Manager of Manufacturing (at the company's Roseau facility) Jeff Bjorkman presented the costing findings to the company's officers.

"We got the okay from the officer group to go to prototype," Parks said. He was happy with the decision but wondered who would do the work. Parks had no official motorcycle-related title, and more importantly, he had no staff.

In the summer of 1994, he and Chuck Baxter (vice president, engineering and product safety) hired some engineers for preliminary chassis and transmission work. "But that was really a waste of time," Parks said. "We got some work done, and we did have some competitive bikes [in hand for evaluation], so we did learn something, but until Geoff Burgess came on board in September of 1994, we didn't get very much accomplished."

Burgess was the third person hired for the Victory project. Considering his leadership and significant contributions to the project, he remains the most significant hire of all.

# CODENAME: VICTORY

When Polaris staff members began their research, working with outside consultants, they needed a code name for the project that would maintain confidentiality.

Parks came up with the Victory name. "Victory came along because it was a nonsensical name with positive connotations," said Parks. "It's a great name, and obviously it stuck. It's 'V for victory.' It's nostalgic; it has World War II connotations. It's as appropriate as 'Polaris' is for snowmobiles, really."

The name of the first Victory model is the V92C. The "V" stands for the V-twin engine, "92" stands for the engine's 92-cubic inch displacement, and "C" stands for cruiser.

"Our main goal right now is to build the brand-name recognition," Parks said. "Instead of calling this model the 'Rapture' or the 'Blackbird,' we called it the V92C. When somebody says, 'What kind of bike do you have?' we want the answer to be, 'I have a Victory.'"

# 2

# BENCHMARKS AND GOALS

## Designing a Greatest Hits Package

Sweating in their leathers in the hot desert sun, Victory staff members learned some valuable lessons early in the project. On an unlikely stretch of road, in full view of the public, they made discoveries. These riders weren't on a secret test track with banked turns and "S" curves or on a drag strip with sensors to monitor speeds and times.

No, they were on a freeway in the heart of Phoenix, Arizona, stuck in rush hour traffic on a hot fall day. The test pilots were members of the Victory and Polaris engineering departments' staffs, and they were riding

*Design of the Victory began after thousands of hours of testing and evaluation, a process known as benchmarking. During 1993 and 1994, the Victory team began the process by thoroughly evaluating the competitors' motorcycles. In addition to evaluating ride and performance, the Victory team disassembled two of the bikes—a 1992 Honda Shadow and a Harley-Davidson FXRS—to weigh and measure nearly every part and component group.*

competitive brands of motorcycles. There, in the insufferable heat, they learned things about how they wanted to design and develop the Victory motorcycle.

They also learned how much you can sweat in black leather and full-face helmets.

What brought them to Phoenix on Hondas, Kawasakis, and the rest of the competition was a design process known as "benchmarking," which consists of evaluating other vehicles to determine the best performance characteristics and features. With such ratings in hand, designers and engineers develop vehicles with the best-possible combination of features at the desired price points.

"We really spent a lot of time riding the other bikes, understanding their pros and cons, and trying to build something that was better," Parks said. "We never tried to copy anybody. We wanted to build something that

*The Victory team extensively road-tested the competitive cruisers—including the Yamaha Royal Star and Virago, Honda Shadow ACE and Valkyrie, and Harley-Davidson Road King—as well as the Ducati Monster and BMW R1100RS. Everything from clutch feel and low-end power to touring comfort and high-speed handling was evaluated and ranked. The best of each category set a benchmark, which became the goal for Victory.*

Once the Victory group's early vision for the bike, the data gathered from benchmarking, and market demands all jelled into firm goals, the Brooks Stevens design group, based in Milwaukee, Wisconsin, was called on to put the team's vision to paper. The hidden fuel system and rear suspension from this March 1995 drawing survived, while the tank-top instruments, Supertrapp-style dual-side exhaust, and upside-down forks were scrapped. Victory

This Brooks Stevens drawing, also dated March 1995, shows a chunkier, taller machine. The fat bob tank, tank-top instrumentation, staggered duals, and crossover tube are retro cruiser, while the scalloped headlight and flared fenders offer a wink and a nod to the 1940s. Victory

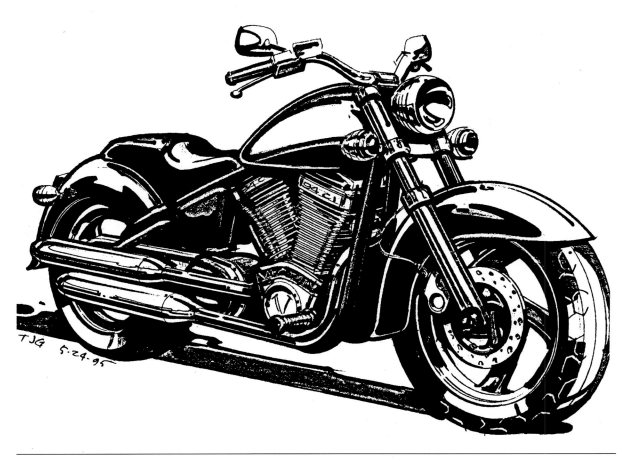

*By May 24, 1995, Brooks Stevens had turned the input of the Victory group into a close approximation of the V92C. Chunky, aggressive lines complement the stout V-twin, while subtle fender flares accentuate the elemental design.* Victory

was better, that had a unique Victory flare, so at the end of the day when a guy says, 'Why should I buy a Victory motorcycle?' we can say, 'How long do you have? We'll tell you.' And if he or she rides it, in five minutes they will know why.'"

## Benchmarking and Data Collection

Victory team members in 1994 purchased a fleet of motorcycles—including cruisers, touring bikes, and sport bikes such as a Ducati—and evaluated every detail of each bike. The bikes (referred to as "competitive" bikes since they came from other manufacturers) were ridden in Minnesota and Tennessee and also extensively in Arizona by Victory team members and Polaris engineering staffers on group benchmarking trips.

During the Arizona trip, when seven competitive bikes were ridden, each rider completed a three-page evaluation form during and after his ride on a bike. The form elicited ratings of all the performance characteristics, ergonomics, and features of each bike. Following the trip, the ratings were compiled to determine the consensus view of the best version of each feature within a class (or market segment) of bike and the best version of each feature overall.

For instance, the Kawasaki Vulcan might have been judged to have the best brake feel among cruisers, while the Ducati had the best acceleration of all the bikes tested.

The Victory team also assessed the cost of producing the best features to determine whether they could combine those features in a bike and still hit the targeted Victory price range.

These steps were all parts of a wide-ranging data-accumulation process that gave the Victory team members a clear vision of what they wanted their motorcycle to consist of

*To evaluate a range of chassis dimensions, the Victory group built this crude prototype called "Francis" in May 1995. Although it was a highly effective tool, the bike's rough appearance raised some eyebrows. "People thought it was a production model," Geoff Burgess said with a laugh.*

*Using input gathered from Francis the Mule, the Victory team transformed the Brooks Stevens design ideas into a detailed computer model. Nearly every single nut and bolt on the Victory was envisioned and created with Vellum and ProE, two computer-aided design (CAD) programs. This image was used for a presentation to the board of directors. Victory*

and whether such goals were fiscally possible. The following data collection methods were used.

As noted in chapter 1, before the Victory project was given the green light, engineers had disassembled and done a cost analysis of every component of a Honda Shadow and a Harley-Davidson FXRS.

Prior to the Arizona benchmarking trip, the Victory team approached Dunlop, the tire manufacturer (and a supplier of Polaris ATV tires), to request information about motorcycle tires. With the help of Steve Paulos, a Dunlop test technician with an impressive motorcycle industry background, the Victory team gathered information about competitive motorcycles. Paulos and some of his industry contacts helped the Victory leaders learn more about competitors' development and production processes—while maintaining confidentiality so the Victory project remained under wraps. Dunlop permitted Paulos to accompany the Victory team on its major Arizona benchmarking trip, and his experience led to his providing valuable insights about the evaluation bikes.

(He later was hired for the Victory team and subsequently became an independent consultant to the Victory project.)

Following the Arizona benchmarking rides, the Victory team disassembled the competitive bikes and weighed and evaluated all of their components. This helped them set a target for the acceptable weight of the Victory model and evaluate component materials and production processes.

## Lessons from the Desert Heat

This data was distilled and analyzed, and the Victory team came up with goals for the bike's makeup. Among the details was the Victory engine's displacement. The Vulcan (which then had a 1,470-cc engine) received the highest marks among cruiser engines on the benchmarking rides; its smoothness, acceleration, torque, and throttle response received high ratings. The Victory team determined it should take things a step further and build an even bigger engine to produce even more power. The team settled on a displacement of 1,507 cc (slightly less than 92 cubic inches). Not overlooked, of course, are the bragging rights gained from having the biggest cruiser engine with the most horsepower on the market for that time.

The western benchmarking trip also contained hard lessons that led to the Victory engine being oil-cooled.

*During the early part of 1996, the Victory computer model became increasingly intricate. With the exterior details and dimensions nearly complete, the engineers sent their CAD drawings to Brooks Stevens, who generated this three-dimensional illustration in the spring of 1996. The V92C was taking shape.* Victory

# PROFILE:
# GEOFF BURGESS

Geoff Burgess' impressive motorcycling background is like a brand-name-dropping feast that could make him popular as a speaker at vintage motorcycle meets and shows the world over. But his job is to develop motorcycles for the future, not linger amid memories of yesteryear.

Turn back the clock to the mid-1960s. Scotsman Burgess worked for the Norton-Villiers Engine Company for about five years, then worked in the Triumph Research Center (part of the Norton-Villiers-Triumph Group, which later included BSA as well). There he met Mike Mills. Like Burgess, Mills has become a key player in the Victory story, but more on him later.

In 1971, the British motorcycle industry, reeling from Japanese manufacturers' rise to market dominance, collapsed. Burgess emigrated to North America, while Mills struck out on his own as a consultant.

Burgess became product development engineer for Monark, a California-based motorcycle importer, and in 1976, he joined Bombardier for a 12-year run that included a stint as director of research and development for Can-Am motorcycles. He eventually went to work for Bombardier's Ski-Doo snowmobile division, but not before once again crossing paths with Mills who worked in the 1980s for Armstrong, a European motorcycle manufacturer. You see, from 1982 on, Can-Am motorcycles were actually Armstrong bikes with Can-Am decals.

After leaving Bombardier, Burgess was an industrial consultant in Montreal, and he sent his résumé to Polaris. The company contracted with him to assist in developing a personal watercraft prototype, but he had been with Polaris only a month when a noncompete clause with his previous employer was deemed a liability.

He worked on four-wheelers—automobiles—with the GM/Delco Advanced Chassis Group in Milford, Michigan, and in 1992, just as GM offered him a position at its tech center in Paris, Polaris called. The Bombardier no-compete period had elapsed, and Polaris had a job to offer.

"As I was about to take the GM job in Paris, France, [Polaris Engineering Vice President] Chuck Baxter called to offer me the job as head of the watercraft project," Burgess recalled. "Whatever my interest might have been, it didn't really matter, because when my wife was faced with choosing between Roseau, Minnesota, and Paris, you know where I ended up."

Oui.

He essentially disappeared in Europe, because when Baxter sought him out in 1993 for the Victory project, none of Burgess' old U.S. contacts knew how to reach him. The search lasted several months.

"I came back to the Milford Proving Grounds in March 1994, and Jeff Smith [an old Bombardier cohort] said, 'Where have you been? Polaris has been looking for you.'"

In September 1994, Burgess joined the Victory team, but only after reaching an understanding with Baxter about how the motorcycle project would proceed. Burgess had helped develop numerous vehicles, using both old and new technologies, and he wanted it understood that the project could not be rushed. He felt thorough analysis and design work were necessary before prototypes were built; he insisted on taking this approach rather than building too-crude mules and trying to shape them into thoroughbreds with welding rods.

At the outset, he sparked progress in the bike's development. As he developed a staff of engineers and designers, he offered direction, input, and freedom, entrusting them with broad responsibility to develop the best motorcycle possible. He served as a manager, teacher, and foremost, a highly talented engineer.

"When Geoff came on board, that's when the work really started going, and we laid out the whole plan for the bike," said Matt Parks.

"Geoff and I worked really hard to define what the motorcycle should be. We had a general idea written up, a marketing plan, and early on Geoff had read that. But he and I had a lot of long sitdown discussions about what the motorcycle should be. We got along real well, and we agreed, pretty much from the start, what it should be. But Geoff is the consummate engineer, and he wanted to do a better job, and he really pushed us to do a better job."

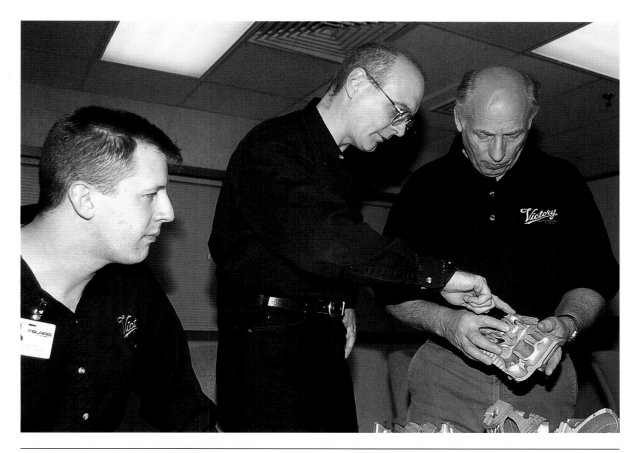

*Geoff Burgess, shown conferring with Mark Bader (center) and Steve Weinzerl (seated), has been building motorcycles for more than 30 years. Experience with Triumph, Norton, and Can-Am, natural instincts for what motorcyclists want, and a frank, open demeanor made Burgess an ideal choice to lead the Victory's engineering team.*

"We were stuck in this horrible Phoenix traffic, trying to get across town because none of us really knew where we were going," Parks said. "It was hotter than hell, 95 [degrees] in the shade and probably 105-plus on the road. Actually, it was one of the better tests we did because we had several bikes that were liquid-cooled, some that were oil-cooled, and several that were air-cooled. On the air-cooled bikes, the cylinders appeared to, for lack of a better word, 'go square,' and these brand-new air-cooled bikes were just billowing smoke. I mean, *billowing* smoke! The fans would go on in the liquid-cooled bikes, and they would keep nice and cool; the heat didn't do anything bad to them. They just sat there and idled in traffic.

"And, interestingly enough, with the two oil-cooled bikes, one of them just acted like it did at any time, and with the other one, the idle went up slightly. But other than that, they behaved themselves quite nicely."

## Getting a Feel for the Handling

The Arizona trip also greatly helped the Victory team define its handling goals.

Geoff Burgess, after riding one cruiser said, "I think that frame just wound up like a spring, and for every action, there's an opposite reaction."

"It had to let go," Parks explained. "Sometimes right when you were deep in the corner, it would kind of release. It was very disconcerting, and we didn't like it."

When such a chassis "uncoiled" in a turn, it gave the rider the unpleasant feeling of fighting the bike rather than riding it, particularly at higher speeds. These cruiser bikes typically had rubber-mounted engines, and the frames flexed more than sport bikes with stiffer chassis.

*The first prototypes with Victory engines are known as C bikes. Although most of these were very roughly finished, the bike shown was painted and finished for a presentation to the board of directors. The engine fins were polished with a belt sander, handmade aluminum pieces hide the bolt holes for the rear seat mount, and the Victory script on the handlebar mount was laser-printed on an overhead, cut out, and glued on. Victory*

The next generation of development bikes was the PD bikes. The major difference between the C and PD bikes was a redesigned frame. This is PD-2, perhaps the only PD bike to use the older C frame.

If the Victory team members had been content to make a cruiser copycat that sold because of its American origin and sharp styling, then a sloppy handling bike with a flexing chassis would have been acceptable. But they set their goals much higher. They wanted to create a cruiser that a rider could really push instead of simply settling in for the ride. They wanted to build a bike that delivered a high-performance ride instead of making riders accept passive, low-speed cornering.

They didn't want riders to have to back off the throttle in tight turns. They wanted the thrill of motorcycling to come from the bike's performance, not from tank badges and a cool line of clothing.

Need proof that excellent handling was the team's top priority? Consider: The chassis and frame were designed as desired, *then* the engine was reconfigured to fit in the available space in the frame (details of this appear in chapter 3).

After the Victory team determined which benchmarked bikes delivered the desired, agile-handling ride, it did a thorough analysis of all the competitive bikes' chassis. The suspensions were dissected, and the chassis were tested for torsional rigidity.

"We measured the stiffness of each bike's chassis," said Burgess. "We compared the stiffness to the feel of the bike's handling. We chose the best [-handling chassis] and designed our chassis to match its [stiffness] number."

The approach was successful. "The first chassis we built essentially handled the way we wanted," Burgess said.

Benchmark riders' subjective ride impressions were used along with the hard data acquired from stiffness testing. The data acquisition equipment obtained accurate information and allowed engineers to compare the objective data against subjective riding impressions.

"We tried to correlate what the seat of our pants had told us first with some of the data acquisition," Parks said. "Once we'd get some actual [stiffness] numbers, we'd say, 'Okay, we did a torsional stiffness test of this frame, and it was really a flexible frame, and that's what we thought when we rode the bike.'

"We realized we wanted a stiff chassis. We wanted a bike that felt like a twin and had a nice low center of gravity but didn't vibrate so bad that your hands would go numb, your feet would go numb, and parts would fall off the bike."

The team also measured and evaluated the bikes' steering geometry. There was a considerable variation in the steering angles (rake) and trail measurements. This data was analyzed in relation to evaluations of how well each bike handled, and target geometries were selected—those expected to deliver the desired Victory handling—so they could be applied to the first test vehicle (see next chapter).

The Victory team took the most thorough, methodical, and analytical approach to the research and development program, so the program didn't waste time, money, or valuable resources. The chassis and frame analysis work was typical of the Victory team's approach to major aspects of the bike, such as the engine and chassis: The team did extensive analysis before ever building prototypes so the prototypes would be as refined as possible from the outset. This resulted in the most efficient and effective development work on the prototypes. It also took advantage of the capabilities of state-of-the-art design and analysis software.

"It was design by mathematics, not by iteration," Burgess said. "Some people weren't comfortable with it. They wanted to see some prototypes, wanted to see us build something, but we took our time and did it right before building anything."

"The entire project has been a fairly rapid development cycle," Parks said. "But a lot of up-front thinking has saved us a lot of time on the back end."

Once the team had collected and analyzed loads of chassis data, "Francis" was created.

---

*The third generation of Victory prototypes was the CV bikes. As with the earlier machines, many subtle changes were implemented. The major changes with the CV bikes took place within the engine. The final preproduction motorcycles were known as P bikes.*

# 3

# LEARNING LESSONS FROM FRANCIS

## In Pursuit of Superior Handling

He was the Gunga Din of the Victory project, the unsung hero who gave all to help develop the V92C. He worked long hours, got dirty without complaint, and proved incredibly adaptable to the engineers' requests.

He never asked for a raise, never showed up late, or never took too long for lunch.

Despite unkempt looks and a definite lack of polish, the contributions he made were invaluable, and he was an unforgettable member of the original Victory team.

In his one concession to chasing star status, he went by a one-word name like Elvis, Madonna, Fabian, and Liberace before him.

*When the road turns curvy, the Victory team's dedication to a rigid chassis pays off. Victory test riders found the competition's cruisers to be soft and unstable in the corners. As a result, chassis stiffness became a priority for the V92C. Who says a crusier has to corner like a 1963 Buick?*

They called him: Francis.

A rolling prototype used in the development of a vehicle, whether it's a car, truck, motorcycle, or ATV, is commonly called a mule. It's a test lab designed to prove or disprove theories, ideas, and settings. A variety of specifications are tried to arrive at one ideal specification. This working beast is long on function and short on styling. It might not be pretty, but it will work long hours, take loads of abuse, and ideally, teach the technicians a lot about the vehicle being developed.

Such was the case with "Francis," the mule used to develop the Victory chassis. (This two-wheeled beast was named after Francis the Talking Mule, the four-legged star of six silly but popular movies produced between 1949 and 1956.)

Antoine Pharamond, a young project engineer straight out of the California aircraft industry, started design work on Francis in

*It ain't pretty, but some of the most critical chassis development was done with this battered beast. Built in May 1995 with a right-hand belt drive V-twin engine and an adjustable chassis, Francis the Mule was used to determine optimum chassis dimensions. The Mule's wheels, Fox shock, and Marzocchi forks made it to later prototypes, while the rubber-mounted engine would be jettisoned in favor of the superior torsional stiffness of a solid-mounted powerplant.*

early 1995. The Victory team developed a chassis that offered the responsive handling it demanded. Francis was the road-going step beyond the computer design and analysis work already done on the chassis. The mule let the team determine the steering geometry needed for a responsive cruiser, learn whether the frame and chassis would meet their torsional stiffness goals, and refine the suspensions.

"The bike was starting to take form on paper," Parks said. "We agreed it should weigh about this much; it should have this; it should have that. At that point, we started building a mule, which basically meant taking the geometry that we had laid out and building this adjustable chassis. The purpose was to learn absolutely as much as we could about the geometry, the seating position, and the ergonomics to make this thing, from a chassis standpoint, be better than cruisers currently on the market."

## Francis Is Born

Pharamond, former Victory technician Jere Peterson, Steve Paulos (originally in charge of Victory testing and development), Parks, and Geoff Burgess developed the Mule

The swingarm pivot location was adjustable, and the bike's center of gravity could also be altered.

Paulos had previously done developmental work for Honda on the six-cylinder Gold Wing and Pacific Coast models. During such projects, the test chassis had not been adjustable, so making chassis geometry changes was much more complicated and time-consuming than it was with Francis.

Describing prior projects, he said, "You had to cut things apart, and when you welded them back together, you weren't sure you weren't changing something else along with what you wanted to adjust."

What was Francis' primary task? To help the team achieve its distinct goals for the Victory ride and handling.

*By adjusting the Mule's crucial chassis dimensions—wheelbase, steering-head angle, rake, trail, swingarm pivot location, and more— the Victory team was able to test major design changes with the twist of a couple bolts.*

in a creative, efficient fashion: The chassis was adjustable. The frame was built with the torsional rigidity the team wanted (based on benchmarking), and select components could be mounted in varied positions.

"The Mule had the desired stiffness built into it, but we could adjust the geometry," Paulos said. "We could change the steering head angle and change the trail and rake, among other things. By only changing one thing at a time we could really evaluate changes."

*Extensive testing of control placement was also done with the Mule. Load cells were mounted on the levers to gather data, while test riders did the same. The results were compared to the data gathered during benchmarking and used to determine leverage ratios and placement that gave the best feel and action.*

"This bike was being designed to really go around a corner, because obviously, people on the team wanted to give their input into the design, and these guys like to ride at a fairly decent pace," Parks said. "I mean, they're not roadracing a cruiser, but they wanted this bike to have real good handling characteristics."

Parks and Burgess compared current cruisers to big, soft-handling luxury cars of another era.

"Geoff and I felt a lot of the cruisers looked good, and they felt good and all that, but their handling was kind of like a mid-1970s luxury car. They kind of had marshmallow handling,"

Parks said. "You wouldn't want to go around the corner *too* fast on this bike, but look where those same [luxury] cars are today—Cadillacs, Lincolns, BMWs, Mercedes, and Lexus. They're fast, have good brakes, and they go around a corner really well. They're much more sporty than they were in the 1970s, and we took the same approach: 'Why *can't* a cruiser go in that direction? Why shouldn't it handle really well?' It would help differentiate us also."

Paulos knew from career experience that a big bike could be designed to handle easily, and today he feels the Victory team succeeded in reaching its handling goals.

*By using an existing engine to power the Mule, Victory engineers were able to develop an ideal chassis before they were committed to the engine design. This slave engine was chosen because the dimensions, integral gearbox, and right-side output shaft matched what was planned for the V92C powerplant. As a result of what was learned from the Mule, the specified length for the Victory engine was shortened more than 15 percent.*

"What we were looking for was something with a light and nimble feel even though it's a 600-pound motorcycle," he said. "I had been so impressed at Honda by how easily the GL1500 [Gold Wing] handled even though it was an 800-pound bike. With the Victory, we developed a confidence-inspiring motorcycle. It doesn't do anything to scare you. As we developed the chassis, I was thinking about the customer, and they're not all experienced riders. I wanted to make it a ride they'd be comfortable with, enjoy, and feel safe."

But that ride was achieved only after Francis rolled up thousands of miles, and the team—and others—logged countless hours in the office and shop.

Although the Victory team worked independently (not sharing staff with other Polaris product divisions), the team received valuable input from some Polaris engineers.

"The Mule was getting really well-defined, and we had some early drawings of the frame, but we were sort of struggling with some frame components, and we got some excellent help from people like Mihai," Parks said of Mihai Rasidescu, a Polaris ATV engineer. Chassis development was also aided by at least two other Polaris engineering staffers: Glen Arneson, a CAD designer, and Guoguang Chen, who provided valuable Finite Element Analysis (FEA) assistance. (The FEA process uses complex computer software to analyze designs and structure to determine stress and load paths in components such as frames. Using FEA software, Victory team members learned where the greatest stresses would be on the frame and chassis components, allowing them to make structural adjustments.)

Mario Negri, a design engineer true to his Italian heritage, had a flair for styling and aesthetic design. He took over from the good foundation work of Rasidescu, Arneson, and

*Steve Paulos oversaw much of the chassis development done with the Mule. Paulos' experience developing the Honda Gold Wing and Pacific Coast was key to the Victory's agile, forgiving handling. Paulos is shown in the original Victory shop in Osceola, Wisconsin, near one of the early CV bikes.*

Chen and turned the frame and swingarm into works of art. Using Chen's FEA findings, Negri was able to reduce the weight of the frame by 20 pounds by the time it was ready for production.

## The Makeup of the Mule

There were two significant reasons why Francis was a test bed only for chassis makeup and handling, not for Victory engine development. First, chassis development was a top priority because of the team's insistence that the bike offer superb handling. Second, at the time, there was no engine design staff. Engine Design Manager Mark Bader hadn't even been hired when Francis was born. Bader was hired in May 1995.

Since no Victory test engine existed in early 1995, when Peterson was assembling

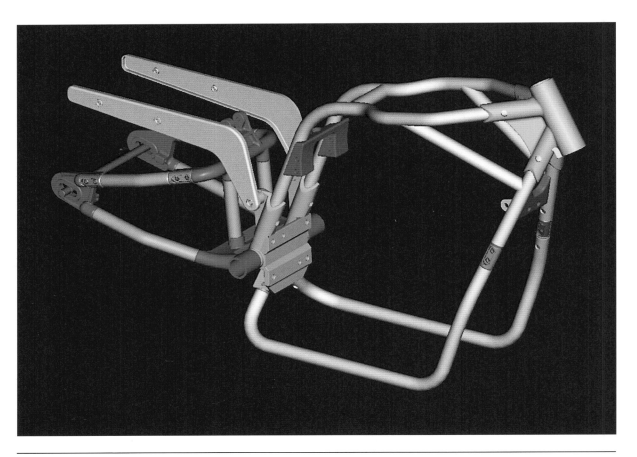

The testing done by Paulos and others with the Mule was translated into the ideal dimensions for the frame. This computer-generated image shows a preproduction version of the frame used on the C bikes and at least one of the PD bikes. The cross-pieces near the steering head are the major giveaway that this is an early frame. Victory

Francis, a "slave" engine was needed. An air-cooled V-twin test engine was installed in the Mule because it had a right-hand side belt drive, as the V92C would have.

"The engine was solidly mounted, so there was a horrible vibration and great frame flex," said Burgess. "The high-speed stability was not great, but it wasn't expected to be, because the frame had bolts everywhere, like Frankenstein's monster."

(At the time, plans still called for the Victory engine to be rubber-mounted, not solid-mounted to the frame. Thus, the Mule wasn't designed to accommodate a solid-mounted engine, and the significant vibration was not a primary concern.)

In contrast to the engine, the Mule's suspension components were very similar to eventual production parts.

"We had our own custom forks, the production forks, so we started to play around with the spring rates and the damping rates on Francis, and then we did the same thing with the rear shock using a Fox shock, which is basically what we're using now," Burgess said.

The Mule's Marzocchi forks had big—for a cruiser—45-mm tubes. By comparison, most cruisers have forks in the 36- to 42-mm range. The Victory team sought the larger forks to ensure that the chassis would have the desired rigidity and, in a marketing move, to earn bragging rights for the biggest forks on the market—at least for the time being.

"The torsional rigidity of the forks is better when you go with the bigger size, so there is an advantage," Burgess said. "Plus, we did a survey, collected the competitors' measurements, and said we want to be bigger than what's out there, because either by the time we're out there, everybody will be at that level, or we'll have an advantage. They're getting bigger and bigger on the market."

Why Marzocchis? In part because a North American source couldn't be found, nor, for that matter, was there a Japanese vendor capable of giving the Victory team the engineering input it sought along with the hard parts.

Burgess recalled, "With my previous connections with Marzocchi from Bombardier, where we had used them in Can-Ams [dirt bikes], we talked to Marzocchi, and they said, 'Oh, yeah, we've got 45-mm Magnum forks. We've won 17 World Championships with

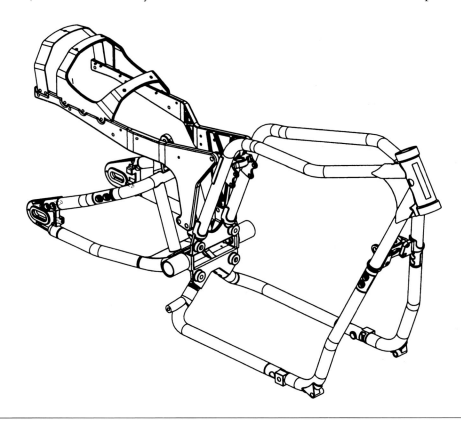

*Once the dimensions of the frame were determined, finite element analysis (FEA) was used to identify key stress points. This allowed the frame to shed about 20 pounds and yet maintain the rigidity required by the Victory team's parameters. The lightened frame was used on most of the Victory preproduction bikes. Victory*

these forks, and we can build you a street version of them.' That's how we ended up with our 45s."

The team got assistance and feedback from Marzocchi's technicians, but the aluminum fork slider is an original Victory concept, as are the triple clamps. These pieces were designed by Lewis Vaughn, an Arizona transplant to Minnesota.

To evaluate existing steering geometries and set target angles for the Victory, the team benchmarked the competition, measuring the rake and trail of numerous bikes, primarily cruisers, and found considerable variation among them.

"We looked at a spectrum of the market, a Kawasaki Vulcan, a [Harley-Davidson] Road King Softail, a Yamaha Virago, probably six different models," Burgess said. "We plotted their rakes and trails on a graph so we had a scatter plot of these points and saw that, 'Wow, these guys are all over the place,' from 32 degrees to 28 degrees rake, with different trails as well."

*Project Engineer Mario Negri (on left) played a key role in creating the Victory's frame. Beginning with the early frame designed by Mihai Rasidescu, Glen Arneson, and Guoguang Chen (which was used on the earliest prototypes), Negri used computer modeling to lighten the frame without reducing rigidity.*

# Riding the Victory

Quick—what images do the words "American performance machine" bring to mind? The pavement-rippling Chevelle SS454 and Boss 429? The race track thunder of Can-Am and Formula 5000 race cars? Perhaps the 1957 Sportster, from the days when Harley-Davidson and high-performance were synonymous. Horsepower through volume is what these machines share.

The Victory cruiser offers a taste of these legendary American icons, with the same big displacement and emphasis on performance. High technology and modern design techniques helped create the cruiser, but the motorcycle's soul is as all-American as a Camaro Z-28.

Swing a leg over and settle into the seat, and you'll find a comfortable, laid-back seating position that is upright enough to allow you to take a corner with enthusiasm. The controls fall easily to hand, with no unnatural seating position or awkward reach for levers or pedals.

Touch the starter, and the engine fires with a satisfying rumble. Twist the throttle, and the fuel-injected V-twin responds with a powerful snort. Engage the wet clutch, drop it into gear, and the strong low-end torque pulls you away with ease. There is plenty of power down low.

When the revs reach the midrange, the Victory's 92-cubic inch, eight-valve V-twin pulls away from the crowd. The exhaust note changes to a ripping midrange howl, as the 75-horsepower engine gets down to business. Don't expect to eat up too many late model sportbikes—although you might get 'em in top-gear roll-on—but the Victory's powerful midrange will leave the V-twin cruiser competition for dead.

Power is strong and satisfying, but I found the chassis more impressive. The twisting canyon road the Victory and I traveled offered 20-mile-per-hour curves and quick switchbacks that allowed the taut chassis to shine. Compared to the soft, gentile offerings of other manufacturers, the Victory feels short, light, and agile. The rigid chassis and aggressive damping rates encourage you to hit the corners a bit quicker, and the bike responds crisply to steering input.

With solid power, a sporting chassis, and a great sound, the Victory team has created the American hot rod of cruisers.

— Lee Klancher

As test rider Cory McWhorter and this preproduction Victory demonstrate, the V92C makes plenty of power. The ample ponies and a stiff chassis combine to make the Victory the American hot rod of cruisers.

The team analyzed the way the numbers for these bikes compared to one another, taking into consideration how each one's handling had been rated during benchmarking rides. The team then settled on targets of 30 degrees rake and 5 inches of trail.

"That's what we found to be the best compromise without too much sacrifice either way," Burgess said.

Why this talk of compromise and sacrifice?

Because the team was actually developing a chassis for two, and perhaps more, different bikes. In the long-range Victory plan, the standard cruiser, the V92C, will be followed onto the market by other cruiser models.

To maximize efficiency in all areas—from engineering and design to purchasing and assembly—the team wanted to make the original

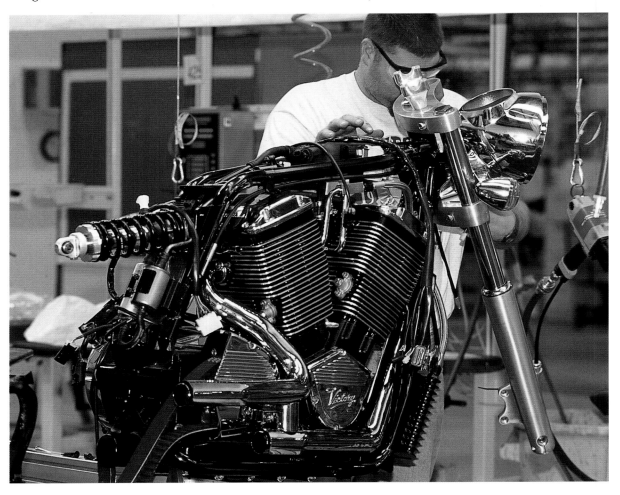

*The Victory frame is a three-piece unit that uses the engine as a stressed member. The backbone of the frame wraps around the top of the engine, providing a main beam of support somewhat similar to the twin aluminum spars used on current sportbikes. The other two pieces wrap around the bottom left and right of the engine.*

Victory chassis adaptable for the second cruiser. They set out to develop a chassis that would initially deliver the desired V92C ride and, with minor modifications, work as the second cruiser chassis. *That's* the compromise they wanted to keep to a minimum, and they feel they have succeeded.

Through testing, team members determined chassis geometry for the V92C model, then developed a setup for the second cruiser by changing the rake, trail, and wheelbase and using different wheels and tires. According to Burgess, they found the median between the two setups and did another check on that to see if they could get the two cruisers to have a common geometry. "We found out we could get enough differentiation between those two models by the suspension and tires and other changes that we'd have between the two, still using the same chassis geometries," he explained.

In fact, Burgess feels that having a chassis with the strengths of each model—the standard cruiser's stiffness and the second cruiser's steering geometry—will make both models better.

"What we've ended up with is a more sporty standard cruiser, and because we have this thick chassis, engine, and forks, I think we're going to end up with a better second cruiser as well."

The V92C has 5 1/4 inches of front suspension travel, more than most cruisers, but that figure includes an allowance for sag-in (the amount the forks compress when a rider sits on the bike), so the usable travel is actually about 4 1/4 inches.

## A Legend's Impact on the Rear Suspension

Some elements of the V92C design were dictated by marketing. After all, despite being unique, the bike had to have *some*

*Early on in the design process, the Victory group went searching for big forks. What they found were beefy 45-mm Marzocchi Magnums that were being used on KTM motocrossers. Shortened and tuned for the Victory, these stout tubes augment the bike's nimble handling. The forks shown are from a CV bike, and the notes were for the test rider's reference.*

traits that are popular with, and familiar to, cruiser enthusiasts. According to Burgess, one such marketing directive concerned the rear suspension.

"Marketing dictated that we have a traditional triangular swingarm without any rear shocks on the outside," he said. "We didn't want twin shocks on the sides."

Familiar with vintage British motorcycles, Burgess suggested a swingarm and suspension setup that dates back to a legendary marque.

*Styling dictated a triangular rear swingarm that mocked the "hardtail" look of the unsuspended bikes of the 1940s. The rider's posterior demands suspension. The simple and effective result was a single shock mounted underneath the seat, with an aluminum subframe supporting the seat and rear fender.*

"We looked at the Vincent, which originally had a dual shock under the seat and ended up with a single shock under there, a mono shock, which, basically, Yamaha copied from Vincent," he said. "We knew that we had to go that route, because that was the only way to get what we wanted without linkages. We didn't want any linkages or anything with a rocker arm setup. We wanted a simple setup—one that worked."

The team used its antisquat goals to determine where to locate the swingarm pivot, and this in turn helped position the final drive, the rearmost section of the driveline.

Burgess said, "We figured out where the swingarm position and, therefore, the gearbox output position, needed to be to get the antisquat number right for the power on and off, throttle on and throttle off."

The rear suspension has 4 inches of travel, about standard among cruisers. The rear shock has a preload adjuster, a threaded collar with which a rider can increase or decrease the preload. Parks, for one, expects few problems with, or complaints about, the rear shock.

"It's got a Fox shock that you would have to pay hundreds of dollars for in the aftermarket to put on another cruiser," he said. "We wanted this high-quality shock to be a standard feature."

Extending toward the rear of the bike—unseen under the rear fender and the seats—is a strong but lightweight aluminum subframe.

"It has quite a lot of load subjected on it when you go through a 'g bump.' There are a lot of g-forces there," Burgess explained, "so we wanted to tie the whole thing together, locate the rear fender and seats, and make sure that we had some integrity. Negri designed a cast-aluminum subframe, and we bolted it on the main frame to minimize distortion, so we can control where the subframe and everything else is going to end up."

He said it was a marketing directive that the subframe's two main arms be covered, not exposed, so they're hidden by the fender. They're also linked for strength.

"We had to tie the two parts together because these things just like to walk around on their own. They're like a 3-foot arm waving around back there. We tied them in with a bracket and some loops in the back to make it a good structure and to be able to put the seats on there so the weight on the seats would be evenly distributed." Super Mario did it again.

## A Resizing of the Engine

Once the frame and chassis took shape, the engine team had to adapt the powerplant to the available space.

The Victory team members are motorcycle people, first and foremost, and they engineered their bike with a number of timeless machines in mind. The legendary Vincent Black Shadow's single shock inspired the Victory's rear suspension design. Jeff Hackett

*During early development of the Victory chassis, test riders knew that something just wasn't right but couldn't seem to find the cause. Taking a cue from the Norton Manx, which aligned the centers of the front and rear axles with the crankshaft, the Victory's crank was dropped one inch. The result? Handling that is pure magic. Doug Mitchel*

"We eventually came up with the engine space, and they had to make the engine fit in the frame," Burgess said. "We shrank the engine to make it fit, yet all critical factors in the power-on and handling dynamics were considered in the locating of the gearbox sprocket. We had to change the engine's V angle from 55 degrees to 50 degrees to get the engine to fit and get the horizontal [rear] shock in place so the cylinders' center-to-center distance grew closer."

Burgess acknowledged that the frame-first development process might be unusual, but he feels it was proper in the case of the V92C.

"It's backwards in terms of timing but not in terms of the design process," he said. "This way we ended up with the chassis and the way to deliver the ride and handling we want rather than letting the engine size determine the bike's size and layout. There was no ride compromise in this process."

The decision to solid-mount the engine in the frame and make it a stressed member (covered in depth in chapter 4) further ensured that the chassis would retain the desired rigidity.

"The original parameter was to rubber-mount the engine," said Mark Bader, who is now the design manager. "The more we looked at that, the more we decided it was a bad idea. The number one reason is that the engine is far stiffer as a unit than the chassis, and it didn't make any sense for us to take the stiffest thing in the bike and isolate it from the frame."

It was believed—correctly, it turns out—that if the engine were solid-mounted, a balance shaft would be required to rein in the vibration the engine produced.

"I said, 'Okay, I can put a balance shaft in there, and we can get rid of all the primaries [vibration frequencies], and we'll just have the [less-substantial] secondaries left, and we can have a much stiffer chassis,'" Bader said.

It also relieved the team of having to learn about, develop, or acquire suitable rubber engine mounts.

Burgess recalled, "The balance shaft, Mark basically drove that, saying, 'We need a balance shaft; that's the only way to go. We don't want that rubber-mounting stuff.' We didn't understand this rubber stuff at all. You read about how Harley-Davidson spent something like 15 years getting it right, and we had to get it right within 2 years. We thought, it was a 'no-brainer' [to solid-mount the engine], so we went with a balance shaft."

## Lessons Learned, Challenges Faced

As it did with other aspects of the bike, the team learned a lot about suspensions and chassis design while developing the bike. Team members feel this on-the-job expansion of their knowledge base equips them to capably develop future bikes and to respond to any problems that arise with production bikes.

"We spent a lot of engineering time understanding the geometry of the rear end," Parks said.

## THE FIRST RIDE

The Osceola, Wisconsin, municipal airport isn't known for its aviation firsts. But it was home to history of another sort—the motorcycling kind—on November 7, 1996, when the first Victory concept bike was ridden on its runway.

A group of 18 people, including Victory team members, Polaris corporate executives, and a couple of selected friends of executives, gathered on the rural runway to see, hear, and feel the company's new baby. Everything went fine, and while there wasn't much of an opportunity to experience the bike's responsive handling, some riders did push the bike to triple digits by the end of the airstrip.

Despite the small crowd and the remote location, spy photos were taken.

"Some guy who had landed his plane at the airport saw this unique bike that was running up and down the runway at 100 miles per hour," said Matt Parks. "He's thinking, 'What's up with that?' Next thing you know, he's out there with this gigantic long lens, snapping spy pics. They never made it to magazines, fortunately. But they made it to some dealers."

What was the biggest challenge faced in developing the entire chassis?

"I would say the linking of the frame to the engine so everything is solid, so we had a good, solid connection and everything lined up," Burgess said. "You know, the engine is built in a separate plant from the chassis, and therefore, we really needed to make sure that all of the castings and brackets came within a proper tolerance, so we knew the thing would mount up solid—without a lever or crowbar!"

Burgess' British motorcycle heritage paid off more than once as the Victory chassis was developed, including the time he encouraged Bader to lower the crankshaft. The Victory team was close to achieving its desired chassis design and handling, but something was off a bit. Burgess dusted off a memory, and it paid off.

"Something I knew from my days at Norton and the famous Manx Norton and the Featherbed frame—which would handle as if it were on rails—was the location of the crankshaft centerline and the axle centerlines," said Burgess. "The Manx had a magic about it, and if you took a Featherbed frame and put another engine in there, it didn't handle the same.

*The Victory team's commitment to a solid chassis rewards the rider with lots of confidence in the curves. Although the bike is not going to challenge the GSXRs, CBRs, and FZRs of the world, it will leave other cruisers in the dust when the road gets tight and twisty.*

*Invented and marketed by Greg McDonald (left), the GMD Computrak precisely measures chassis dimensions such as rake, trail, wheel offset, and much more by triangulating a number of data points on the motorcycle's wheel and frame. The Computrak unit functions as a quality control device and will be used in chassis development of future models.*

"The magic was supposed to be that if you had all three gyroscopes in line, it worked," he continued. "So, in other words, the center of the front wheel, the center of the crankshaft, and the center of the rear wheel were in line, and this was supposed to be some sort of a miracle magic. I told Mark about this, and we dropped the centerline of the crankshaft 1 inch to accommodate that, while still keeping the ground clearance. We moved the sump up a bit so we didn't compromise the ground clearance at full bump.

"That is one of the key parameters, I feel, one of the reasons that we have a good-handling chassis. It was just sort of an idea that, 'Wow, I've

heard about this. Let's see what the magic number is and make it like that.' It worked. We were [previously] an inch higher than what we thought we should have been [with the crankshaft centerline]."

Bader cites that alignment as the reason the bike feels light and maneuverable in corners. "A lot of that is attributable to a low center of gravity, and that's all pushed by having that crankshaft below the wheels' centerline. It's slightly below; it's not a lot; it's not an inch below; it's a couple millimeters below, but it is below that centerline, and it makes a huge difference in how the bike feels."

# 4

# MOLDING THE MUSCLE

## Developing a Big-Bore V-Twin from Scratch

After an exhausting week of long hours packed into frantic days, the Victory team stood on a brink. Not just the brink of physical collapse because of sleep deprivation, but on the brink of tremendous accomplishment.

It also stood on the brink of danger—real physical danger.

Motorcycle designers and engineers aren't fire jumpers or Navy SEALs; they're not typically risking life and limb day-to-day—but in the summer of 1996, the Victory staffers who walked into the engine dyno cell walked up to a potential disaster.

On the one hand, they might succeed with the first-ever start-up of a Victory-produced engine. On the other hand, the big, rough, early engine prototype might explode, transforming the developmental tool into a shrapnel-hurling antipersonnel bomb.

Had they thought it through, the men in the cell might have stepped outside behind a wall offering greater protection.

But they were probably just too damned exhausted to walk from here to there. Besides, there was an engine to start and history to be made.

### A Domestic Powerplant

In the early stages of the motorcycle project, the Victory staff determined the bike must excel in two key performance areas—handling and power. Marketing studies told General Manager Matt Parks that the engine had to be a big V-twin, and it had to be U.S.-made; an

*Although the Victory group seriously considered going to outside vendors for engine design, Polaris Engine Design Manager Martin Heinrich helped convince the group it was possible to do it in-house. The 91.92-cubic inch result uses ports designed by wizard Mike Mills (who also worked on Kenny Roberts' Modenas KR3 Grand Prix race bike). With 75 rear-wheel horsepower on tap, test rider Cory McWhorter easily roasts the Victory's 160/80 Dunlop Elite.*

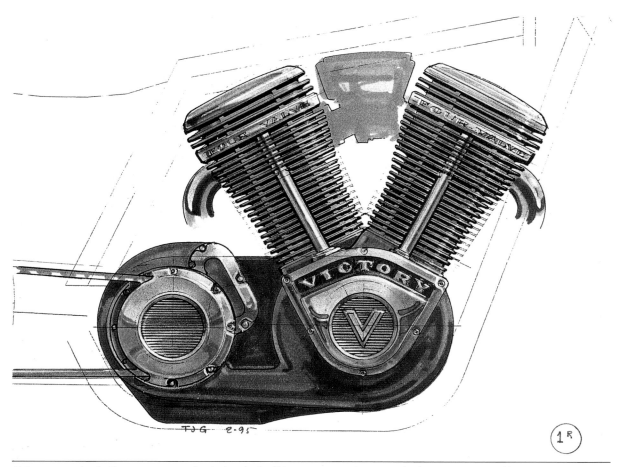

*The parameters for the Victory engine were first laid out by Geoff Burgess in November 1994. The design was massaged by Victory engineers, and in February 1995 Brooks Stevens created this concept drawing. Note the exposed pushrods, which were dropped when the decision was made to go with a single overhead cam. Victory*

American company like Polaris couldn't import the engine for a bike whose targeted buyers love the red, white, and blue imagery of the cruiser culture. The timing of the Victory project was fortunate, because Polaris in the early 1990s was considering starting its own engine manufacturing operation.

A little background: From the mid-1960s until 1995, every Polaris snowmobile and watercraft engine came from Fuji Heavy Industries, a Japanese supplier, and Polaris

ATV engines came from Fuji or from Robin Manufacturing, a Wisconsin-based joint venture between Polaris and Fuji.

Since Polaris first purchased snowmobile engines from Fuji in the mid-1960s, the two companies had built a long and lucrative relationship. It wasn't dissatisfaction with Fuji or its product that led Polaris to consider a domestic engine project in the 1990s. Rather, it was a combination of factors, both positive (the chance for total design, development, and manufacturing control over engine projects) and negative (the volatile exchange rate between U.S. and Japanese currencies).

Polaris continues to rely on Fuji as a major engine supplier but has proceeded with its engine project. The first domestically produced Polaris engines were used in 1996 watercraft and 1997 snowmobiles. The engine project has been successful from the outset; the watercraft and snowmobile engines have received high praise from the media, and models using these engines are strong sellers.

Engine assembly takes place at the company's Osceola, Wisconsin, facility, which,

in December 1995, became home to the Victory engine team after it was decided that's where the Victory engine would be built—not only in the United States, but by the company itself.

## Engine Alternatives

It wasn't always certain that the Victory division would design its own engines. In fact, Victory team members Burgess and Parks traveled to Europe in March 1995 with members of the Polaris engineering department, including Chuck Baxter, vice president of engineering, to evaluate potential engine design houses.

*Engine designer Mark Bader came onboard in May 1995 to turn parameters into horsepower. While Bader began designing the engine on the computer screen, consultant Mike Mills was enlisted to ensure that the powerplant not only made ample horsepower, but also had the potential for more.*

In England they visited Lotus (the sports car maker and former Formula 1 race team), Cosworth (which produces Indy car and F1 engines for Ford), and Triumph, the motorcycle manufacturer for whom Burgess worked in its first life. (Production of "original" Triumphs ceased in 1982, but the name changed hands, and production of new-generation Triumphs started in 1990.) In Italy they visited Ducati and Aprilia, and in Germany they visited BMW.

"Cosworth had built a Norton engine in the 1970s," Burgess said. "We wanted to look into getting engine design help from either Cosworth or Lotus. The potential bill from Cosworth was enormous, much too costly, and Lotus was very cagey. We figured out they were working on someone else's engine.

"At each stop on the trip, we examined the manufacturing techniques and evaluated whether they could produce what we were looking for," Burgess said. "At that time we were still asking who was going to design the engine and who was going to build it."

At Baxter's direction, the team benchmarked engines made by Fuji and Cosworth, from BMW and Kawasaki motorcycles, and the Dodge Neon for manufacturing and assembly insights.

Why benchmark a Neon?

"This was a new generation for Chrysler, and they had some really neat ways they drove the camshaft and the way they mounted it," Burgess said. "They minimized the mass of the engine. It was good to look at the technologies they had. A lot of it wasn't compatible with a motorcycle engine, but it showed they did something different. They thought outside the box, and it was good to look at that."

One consideration was to have Cosworth provide cylinder head design. The Victory team would do as much engine development as possible and learn what Burgess called "the technology of engine design" through its contact with Cosworth and work on the first engine. The potential flaws in that approach were considerable. The Victory team wouldn't learn all the intricacies of engine design and, the second time around, would continue to depend on an outside supplier or make mistakes experienced designers would avoid.

"We thought that, long-term, we needed to develop an internal competency of engine design and engine development," Parks said.

Thus, the engine was approached with a hands-on, "let's learn how to do this ourselves" approach. That gave the team first-hand design experience that enables it to sort out potential problems and to design subsequent Victory models.

On November 16, 1994, Geoff Burgess explained the intial engine parameters to Martin Heinrich, the Polaris engine design manager, and the Victory team. Heinrich, who joined Polaris in the early 1990s, was a major impetus behind the company's domestic engine program. He helped convince—and show—the company it could design and develop its own engines and that engine production capabilities were within its grasp and budget. Regarding the motorcycle project, he reasoned that since the company would soon produce two-stroke engines, it could expand the engine program and also build four-stroke motorcycle engines.

Burgess' description was the first version of "VICTORY Cruiser four-stroke engine design specifications," a list of specs that would be revised several times as the engine was discussed and designed.

The original Victory V92C projection was a 75-horsepower (at 4,300 rpm) engine.

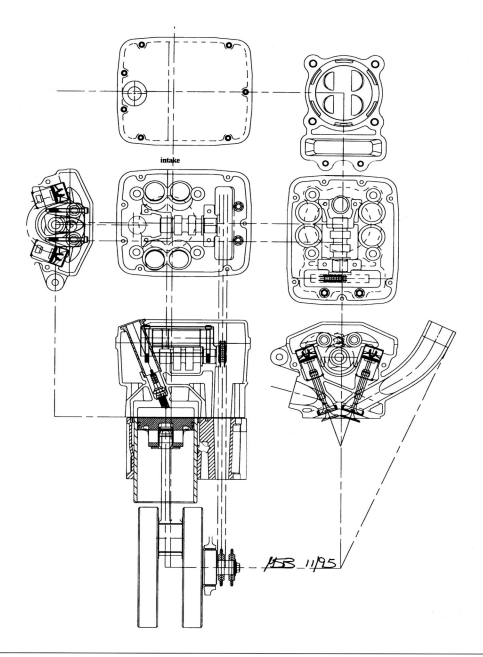

intake

Mike Mills' input was key to the Victory's substantial horsepower. Two of Mills' crucial designs are visible in this Bader drawing from November 1995. Mills drew from his high-performance experience to direct the angle and shape of the ports, vital ingredients for the high-volume flow necessary for big horsepower. Mills also proposed offset rocker arms that would move the single cam over enough to allow the spark plug to be mounted centrally and close to vertical.

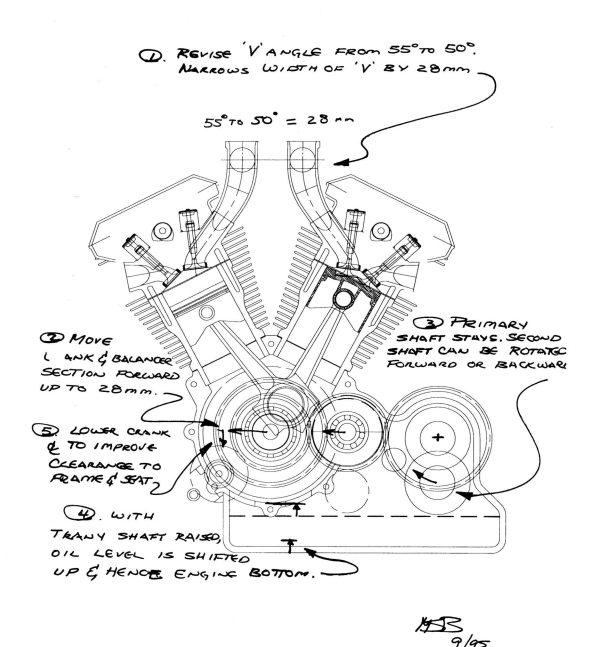

① REVISE 'V' ANGLE FROM 55° TO 50°. NARROWS WIDTH OF 'V' BY 28mm

55° TO 50° = 28 mm

② MOVE CRANK & BALANCER SECTION FORWARD UP TO 28mm.

③ PRIMARY SHAFT STAYS. SECOND SHAFT CAN BE ROTATED FORWARD OR BACKWARD

⑤ LOWER CRANK & TO IMPROVE CLEARANCE TO FRAME & SEAT.

④ WITH TRANY SHAFT RAISED, OIL LEVEL IS SHIFTED UP & HENCE ENGINE BOTTOM.

KSB
9/95

*In the fall of 1995, research done with the Mule demonstrated that the top of the engine needed to be narrowed by about 28 mm to optimize the Victory's handling. This September 1995 engine drawing shows Bader's proposed modifications to narrow the engine.*

*By the summer of 1996, the Victory team had the top-end parts it needed to test the engine but was waiting for crankcases. The team decided to have heavy-duty, simplified engine cases carved from a 350-pound block of aluminum billet. The result became known as the "Hammer."*

Among the original, projected specifications were these:

- 97-mm bore, 102-mm stroke, 1,507-cc, bore/stroke ratio of 0.95
- V angle of 55 degrees between cylinder centerlines
- pushrod OHV, four valves/cylinder, solid lifters
- exhaust pipe exits to be on same side
- balance factor TBD [to be determined] in chassis, no balancer, engine to be rubber-mounted in frame . . .
- air-cooled
- fuel supply by carburetors
- two engine mounting points, swingarm and front

Burgess recalled, "We also assessed the risk factor—the potential of achieving the engine goals versus the schedule and under a specified cost—and 'missing technologies.' That is, whether the required manufacturing processes were available to us in the industry." At the time, Burgess rated the risk factor as "low" and the missing technologies as "none."

The Victory engine specifications changed, of course, but the team didn't make a complete U-turn; it simply changed course in some areas. Some examples: Pushrods were never used; the

# THE HAMMER

It was the summer of 1996, and the clock was ticking. The deadline for the Victory team to build and test its first engine was approaching. Parts were coming in from vendors, including the all-important cylinder heads, but the crankcases were running late and wouldn't arrive for another month. That was too long to wait, according to Mark Bader, who was then in charge of engine design.

"Instead of delaying the start-up of the engine, we came up with the idea of creating a simplified engine: no transmission, just the crankshaft, balance shaft, oil pump, and the output shaft. We quickly designed up a very simple crankcase and got a CNC [computer numerically controlled] machine house to start hogging out big old chunks of aluminum."

Hogging out of what? Out of an enormous block of aluminum, that's what.

"The crankcase started out as a 350-pound block of aluminum, and it ended up weighing 30 pounds, so you figure out how many chips we ended up with," Bader said. "A lot of beer cans died for those cases."

Walls that would be 5-mm thick on a production casting were as much as 20-mm thick in the Hammer's cases. "You could light a bomb off inside of these things and not get hurt," Bader said.

The Victory staff worked long hours assembling the Hammer—as well as preparing the brand-new engine dyno. There were struggles with the engine, the dyno, and the mating of the two prior to that hoped-for first start-up. Several 14-hour-plus days later, the crew finally believed the big day had arrived.

"I think we were zombies by that point," Bader said. "Mike Ball was turning the key, and I was in the dyno cell. I think it was Roger (Peterson) and me standing in there. Roger turned to me and said, 'Man, I'm as nervous as when my kids were born.' And I said, 'Yeah, but when your kids were born, there wasn't the chance that they'd blow up and kill you.'"

The first time Ball tried starting the engine, it didn't fire. The team checked for spark and for fuel and determined that the injection system had to be purged so the fuel could reach the injectors.

At 5:45 P.M. on Friday, September 6, 1996, Ball tried the starter again, and the Hammer roared to life.

"It fired right up, and I don't think there was a dry eye in the house," Bader said. "There were high fives and clapping and cheering. Probably what made it more emotional was that we were so doggone tired. It was an awesome feeling standing there. People were just dumbfounded."

The work of managers, engineers, and technicians, such as Scott Walter, Danny Fredrickson, Kevin Hamann, Burgess, Parks, Bader, Ball, and Peterson had roared to life. It was a milestone, but one that came early on what the team has called "The Road to Victory." The bike was far, far from finished but what a thrilling step they had taken that fall Friday.

*After only a few minutes of cranking the engine over, an exhausted, elated Victory team first heard the ear-splitting roar of the unsilenced Hammer at the Osceola, Wisconsin, shop.* Victory

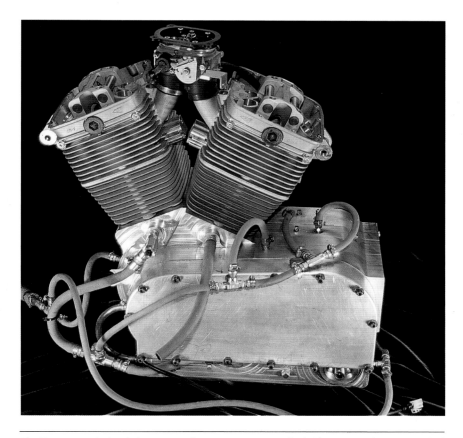

*The Hammer was built only for testing. It has no transmission or clutch. The cases are four times as thick as production units. "You could light a bomb off in those things," Bader said, "and not get hurt."*

exhaust outlets are positioned front and rear, and the engine is fuel-injected, oil-cooled, solid-mounted, and uses a balance shaft.

## Engine Design Gets Rolling

Engine development accelerated, once a staff concentrating solely on the engine was assembled, starting with the May 1995 hiring of Mark Bader to head up engine design. Bader, a former Kohler engine designer, took the original engine parameters and began revising and refining the engine makeup. He was also charged with hiring the engine staff and started in June 1995 with Scott Walter, a former designer for

Carrier refrigeration company who made valuable contributions to the Victory engine.

"Scott was an enthusiastic guy, but he came from Carrier and had done heating units, but he had never designed an engine before," Bader said. "He is an extremely hard-working guy, though, and he had roadraced motorcycles. It was basically just the two of us working on the engine until we moved to Osceola. Scott and I pounded out a tremendous amount of work in the first six months."

The engine—which consists of about 340 parts—was always projected as a high-powered big-bore V-twin, and that didn't change.

The engine retained its original bore and stroke of 97x102 mm; the displacement held firm at 1,507 cc (91.92 cubic inches), and the V angle became 50 degrees.

The cylinders have Nicasil bores, which are effective at transferring heat out from the combustion chamber, and the oil-cooling jackets are concentrated toward the top ends of the cylinders, near the combustion chambers. The pistons are lightweight and have short skirts, and the connecting rods are stout and made of steel. Remember, the idea was to have a modern engine that was powerful and unique.

## It's Cooler with Oil

As noted earlier, the Arizona benchmarking trip led to the team's decision to use oil as its cooling medium rather than water or a traditional coolant-water mixture. The switch to oil cooling posed no major design problems. The 6 quarts of oil are used for cooling and lubrication, and the oil is circulated by dual oil pumps driven by balance shaft gearing. The oil is exposed to cooling airflow in the frame-mounted oil cooler.

Following Death Valley, California, testing, the team increased the size of the oil cooler by about 30 percent, but that has been the biggest cooling system design change since the concept stage. Steve Weinzerl, development manager for engines, said that during follow-up tests using the larger cooler, the Victory engine achieved team cooling goals even in 100-degree-plus desert heat—while pulling a sidecar loaded with test equipment.

The oil's cooling efforts are complemented by each cylinder's 21 cooling fins. The fins transfer heat and direct airflow to the cylinder body.

## SOHC Displaces Pushrod Plan

The original concept of using pushrods to control the valves didn't last long. The idea gave way early in the engine design process to a single overhead cam (SOHC) setup.

"This is a modern engine design that's going to last 10 or 15 years into the future, and pushrods are not what we want," Bader said.

The engine team's challenge: Design a SOHC layout without increasing the engine height. After all, the engine was already packing the allotted frame space. Also, Parks said he didn't want to see external signs that might give it a foreign-made appearance.

The engine height was preserved by sinking the cams low in the heads, something Bader had worked on with a Kohler engine just prior to joining Polaris, so the approach was fresh in his mind.

The cams are controlled by chains that are driven by the crankshaft and hidden in tunnels built into the cylinder walls on the right side of the engine. Since the cooling fins run top-to-bottom on the cylinders, they help mask any external sign of the tunnels. In keeping with the goal of an exceptionally low-maintenance engine, the cam chain tensioners are self-adjusting.

In each cylinder head, a cam controls two rocker arms, and each arm has a twin-pronged roller rocker to activate two valves apiece (two intake, two exhaust) and no-maintenance hydraulic lifters. The spark plug in each head is accessible (using a standard socket) via a tube-like opening in the head casting.

"In a perfect world, you want the spark plug pointed straight up and down," Bader said. "With a dual OHC, you can do that. With our single OHC, we had to miss the cam," so the spark plug sneaks in under the cam at an angle.

Because the engine is solid-mounted and a stressed member of the bike's chassis, standard gaskets can't be trusted to endure the chassis loading. Thus, laminated steel gaskets are used for the head gasket, base gasket, and valve cover gasket. The steel gaskets held up well during all forms of engine testing and, unlike traditional gaskets, aren't prone to creep or deteriorate over time.

The engine's mounting points, which triangulate the stress and load paths, are on the cylinder heads and at four points on the crankcase. The engine is also attached to the cradle at the base of the frame.

## A British Flavor to Heads and Ports

Invaluable input on the port designs came from Mike Mills, an independent consultant from England whom Geoff Burgess has known for years and has worked with previously. Mills is a vastly experienced engineer and designer, and his work on the Victory V-twin was significant because the port shapes and angles were

While the Hammer's cases were one-off CNC units, the heads were essentially production-tooled. The oil-cooling passages are similar to those used on water-cooled bikes. Note the offset placing of the valvetrain and the chambers where the overhead hydraulic lifters rest.

*By August 1996, an engine was installed in C-3, an early preproduction bike. The engine was a paper tiger—literally. Created from CAD drawings using the Victory rapid-prototyping machine, it was made of thousands of precisely cut pieces of paper glued together. Known as LOM parts, these computer-generated mock-ups allow parts to be generated and test-fit without the excessive cost of CNC parts. Victory*

among the most subjective aspects of the engine. It's not so much that there's a right way or wrong way to design ports; rather, they're most aptly judged as being good, better, or best, and the Victory team feels its port flow is among the best possible for this engine. Flow bench tests confirm they're achieving highly effective flow through the heads.

"We decided Mike [Mills] would do the initial head concept, especially for airflow," Burgess said. "Mike would design where the valves went with the included angle, the size of the valves, and the port shapes to get the power that we needed."

Throughout the project, Mills presented his work in pencil drawings, not computer-aided design (CAD) illustrations.

Burgess, for one, felt that was totally appropriate for the design work being done. "Port design," according to Burgess, "is an interpretive, creative process. The design station only does what it's told. The individual has to come up with the better idea, and from there it'll flow. And Mike said, 'This is the only way, because I can rub it out and change it in two seconds.' And you can't do that with ProE design software."

(Mills has since grown familiar and comfortable with design software, which he will use on future Victory projects.)

Mills is more accustomed to working on ultra-high-performance engines, such as those for Kenny Roberts' Grand Prix racing team, than on street bikes. Yet he found it easy to adapt his design approaches to the large-scale cruiser engine.

"Yes. What I know still applies here. All the knowledge you acquire, it still applies.

*Assembly of the Hammer began on September 2, 1996. The Victory group put in a grueling string of 18-hour days over Labor Day weekend to get the first Victory engine hooked up and on their dyno. Victory*

*A lot of sleepless nights put the Hammer in the dyno room at Osceola, Wisconsin, on September 6, 1996. The air was electric that day, prompting Roger Peterson to say, "Man, I'm as nervous as when my kids were born." Bader replied, "Yeah, but when your kids were born, there wasn't the chance they'd blow up and kill you." From left to right are Mike Ball, Peterson, Matt Parks, Jere Peterson, Bader, and Craig Kenfield. Victory*

You're still seeking that efficiency of engine performance," he said. "But you Americans have a funny way of doing things. When you want to go faster, you make it bigger. There's too much mass with all these cruiser engines, but the layout is a marketing requirement. Without marketing input, my cruiser wouldn't look like this cruiser."

## EFI Survives Teething Problems

"Electronic fuel injection on four-strokes was totally new to Polaris," said Steve Weinzerl. Indeed, the company had previously used it only on two-stroke snowmobiles, never on ATVs, the division from which Weinzerl transferred to join the Victory team.

Yet they forged on in the name of progress and developed—with help from a company called MBE that supplies the electronic control unit (ECU)—a fuel injection system that serves the 92-cubic inch engine well.

The original EFI component supplier, whose ECU was used on the first concept bikes, withdrew suddenly in the midst of the project, and most suppliers were reluc-tant to sign on because of the incredibly short development schedule. But the MBE staff's background is in racing, where solutions are needed yesterday, and staffers welcomed the challenge.

"Jeff Moore of MBE was real helpful, and I think it's been a perfect marriage between a vendor and Victory," Weinzerl said. Moore (the "M" of MBE) spent months with Victory team members in Wisconsin, Colorado (for

*On Saturday, October 26, 1996 the first complete Victory engine ran on the dyno at 3:31 P.M. Once again, a string of 18-hour days was required to get engine number C-1 up and firing. As Steve Weinzerl commented, "When you're building the first new American motorcycle to appear in 50 years, you put in a lot of 14-hour days." Mark Bader*

high-altitude EFI calibration), and California, where he helped finalize calibrations before a preliminary emissions test.

The Victory team installed its first EFI setup on the "Hammer," the raw, original Victory test engine (see sidebar). The engine got fuel, started, and ran, but in a sense, it was a case of ignorance serving as bliss.

"Based on what we later learned about EFI, it's a miracle that engine ever started," Bader said. "It probably shouldn't have."

In its production form, the Victory V92C EFI system feeds the engine via 44-mm throttle bores, one per intake port. Just how much fuel is supplied and how fast is controlled by the ECU, which is housed below the seat on the right side of the bike. The ECU isn't a free-thinking brain, however; it had to be programmed with fuel maps that equip it to respond instantly as fuel needs change. Early fuel mapping was done with the V-twin on the engine dyno in Osceola. The second stage

*The next step toward the Victory was to put the engine and chassis together for the first test ride. This historic ride took place on November 7, 1996, at the Osceola, Wisconsin, Municipal Airport. Victory C-1 ran strongly, running up to over 100 miles per hour before the day was done. The early production machine shown is C-3, a finished C bike with an engine installed but not yet running.*

*The bizarre equipment mounted on this early production bike was used for sound testing. By heavily muffling the intake and exhaust noise, the potential for sound deadening could be determined. The odd canister mounted to the rear of the bike would be hooked up to the exhaust pipe during testing. On the left side, a flexible aluminum tube runs from the intake to the front canister. Victory*

of mapping resulted from tests with the bike on a chassis dyno in which the engine performance is measured off the rear wheel. (Both dynos were operated by Senior Development Technicians Roger Peterson and Kevin Hamann who spent thousands of hours in the dyno room during V92C development.)

Final fuel map refinements were made on the road—literally. Here's a typical scenario of how the fuel calibrations were adjusted during field testing: With Weinzerl or Peterson riding the test bike, Moore—in a rough but functional Czechoslovakian sidecar—monitored fueling activity on a laptop computer. The laptop was wired to test equipment that included lambda sensors on both cylinders of the Victory engine. When a fuel supply inefficiency was detected, Moore altered the fuel mapping. Sometimes the adjustments were typed into the laptop on the fly, while other times—such as on rough or twisty roads—the driver pulled over so Moore could type while stationary. The test conditions were then duplicated to verify that the change was effective.

Among the many factors to which the ECU must be able to respond are altitude, driving styles (such as sudden or gradual changes in throttle position, both on and off the gas), and ambient operating temperatures. That's why extensive testing was done at high elevations and in desert heat.

The other ingredient in the induction process, the Victory engine's air intake, is located above the engine, under the gas tank. Thus, unlike most current cruisers, there's no side-mounted air cleaner. The intake's position was chosen for several reasons: to let the tank act as a shroud and slightly muffle intake noise, to provide the bike with clean styling and give it a unique look, and for performance.

"By not putting it on the side, we aren't copying anybody, and it seemed to be best for power because you have a down flow," Burgess said. "The intake ports can be vertical,

*Parts for preproduction vehicles such as this old warhorse, PD-2, are made by creating a CAD drawing and sending it—along with a boatload of money—to a CNC house that turns the computer file into a finished part. Geoff Burgess shook his head and laughed while looking at PD-2, saying, "Can you believe it cost $250,000?"*

*The PD series of preproduction Victories were used mainly for engine testing, although early examples like this one most likely played a role in chassis testing as well. Note the sand-cast side covers, which don't bear the cast logos and polished finish of production units. The spark plug caps on the pipes were reserved for oxygen sensors used during EFI testing.*

*The jumble of wires on the right was used to connect PD-2 to the sidecar rig for EFI testing. The gas tank is made of aluminum, and the engine side cover is an early unit quickly designed by Mark Bader and Matt Parks. The pop can was an economical preproduction breather catch tank.*

as they should be, the way they are on Formula 1 cars, instead of coming from the side, where there's a 90-degree bend into the port. But we had the typical design trade-off and conflict. We had to trade off the hole under the gas tank that eats up space for fuel for the minimum angle we needed to get air into the engine."

## Cranking Out the Inertia

Two major considerations during crankshaft development were space constraints and the need to achieve a targeted level of inertia (an object's ability to maintain its

motion). The team benchmarked crankshafts from numerous competitive motorcycles, measuring the inertia of each one and comparing that data to the particular bike's performance. The team then set inertia goals suitable for its engine's torque and horsepower goals.

"You can get inertia one of two ways, either by diameter or by width of the crankshaft flywheels, so basically when we dropped the crankshaft centerline down, that probably influenced the diameter we could get, so we added the width," said Burgess. "As you can see, the whole engine

The size and shape of the crankshaft helped determine the crankcase size and, thus, overall engine size. The crankshaft connects directly to the balance shaft, an item that wasn't originally part of the plan but which became vital.

## Striking a Balance

In the perfect world, there is imperfection. Without it, things just don't seem right. Babies cry, wagon wheels squeak, blue jeans fade, and cruiser motorcycles vibrate.

Without their familiar vibration—which a rider feels as he straddles a massive V-twin engine caged in a mere motorcycle frame—cruisers just wouldn't feel right.

To the Victory team, that vibration is a part of a cruiser's soul, its mystique, and its image. The vibration is a signature of the

*PD-2's dash is a jumble of parts-store gauges monitoring fuel and oil pressure, yellow temperature sensor leads, and CNC manufactured perches and levers. Tuning notes were made on the strip of duct tape on the tank. The lead hanging from the right control is a throttle position sensor used for EFI testing.*

*One of the biggest challenges the Victory team faced was tuning the EFI. Steady-state testing of the MBE Systems unit was done on the dyno. Several different size throttle bodies were experimented with, and the initial thought was that the engine would work best with a 40-mm body. Dyno tests proved the 44 mms to be the strongest performers.*

was evolving around these magic key elements, which, if you don't have in the first place, you'll never get there."

Bader explained why a big flywheel is a plus in a cruiser.

"In this cruiser market, a lot of times you have low-speed running, in-town running, and you want the engine to be easy to drive at low speeds. That big flywheel helps because it's less susceptible to stalling once you are going. You can basically sit there at no throttle and let it idle its way through traffic."

bike's power, and even though the team found it could eliminate virtually all traces of that vibration, it refused to do so.

The team didn't want to rob the Victory of its soul.

## The Need for Solid Mounting

When the Victory team members decided to solid-mount their engine and make it a stressed member of the frame, they created more work for themselves.

They felt they *had* to solid-mount the engine because rubber-mounting would result in unacceptable frame and chassis flex. After all, one of their key goals had been a stiff, responsive chassis. To permit the engine to shift about and flex the frame would have been self-defeating.

"If you draw a straight line from the steering head to the rear swingarm pivot, it goes right through the engine," said Matt Parks. "What's the strongest piece on the entire motorcycle? It's the engine, a big huge hunk

*Once steady-state EFI tuning was finished on the dyno, this sidecar rig was used to tune the MBE fuel injection system in real-world conditions. Tuning an EFI system is no small task. Burgess estimates the team spent six months or more getting it right.*

With Steve Weinzerl or Roger Peterson driving, Jeff Moore from MBE spent countless hours in this sidecar rig, using a laptop computer to adjust the ECU's fuel map. The fuel map is a set of programmed instructions that control how much fuel is supplied under varying conditions. The olive green lambda monitors display oxygen sensor readings.

of aluminum. We said, 'Let's use this thing as a stressed member.'"

Solid-mounting the engine, however, meant the team had to account for the substantial vibration the engine would transmit throughout the bike. There *are* cruisers with solid-mounted engines and no apparatus to counter the vibrations, but benchmarking rides on such models had resulted in numb thighs and hands as shaky as an espresso addict's.

The answer was a balance shaft that would counter, or neutralize, the vibrations.

## "Tuning" the Vibration

Believe it or not, some people like things that are imperfect, such as lumpy mashed potatoes or, to be more germane, rumbling, vibrating motorcycles. Cruiser riders in particular don't want their bikes to be silent and vibration-free. There's some appeal (and an accompanying image) to a bike that literally makes the ground shake.

This desire for imperfection is an area where some Japanese cruisers fail: They're considered too technologically slick, too quiet

The yellow temperature sensors indicate that this bike was used for cooling system testing. The oxygen sensors tapped into the exhaust pipes are connected to lambda monitors in the sidecar. When the monitor reads "1.00," the oxygen sensors are reading a perfect mixture of 13.7 parts air and 1.0 parts fuel.

or smooth-running, without soul, or even "like riding a Toyota Corolla," which isn't offered as a compliment. The Victory team shared some of these views; some Japanese cruisers struck them as too sterile and free of that desirable cruiser grittiness, while some Harley-Davidsons went too far in the other direction.

That's why the team worked so hard on "tuning" the vibration it *left in* its motorcycle. Bader was familiar with balance shafts, which had been used on virtually every Kohler single, so he was comfortable designing the Victory balance shaft. But it worked too well, in a sense, because it removed virtually *all* of the perceptible vibration, leaving the rider with a too-smooth, sterile ride.

In layman's terms, an engine produces countless vibrations of varying degrees, or frequencies. The only vibrations that merit attention are the first two levels, the primary (major) and secondary (minor) vibrations, because the others are practically negligible.

"We had balanced it to what we thought would be perfect primary balance, so we had just our secondaries, and we really didn't like it," Bader said. "That's because the trick that the equations don't show is that the engine is solid-coupled to the chassis, and the chassis has its own natural frequency, or as a unit, the bike has a natural frequency. The secondary balance that we were experiencing was exciting the natural frequency in the frame, and that made it feel worse than it was. So, by actually *im*balancing the engine more, or further from perfect, it felt better to the rider."

The balance shaft has proven versatile, as it drives the dual oil pumps and serves as an intermediate shaft between the engine and the gearbox. "It's the basis of the gear reduction between the crankshaft and transmission," said Bader.

Originally, the transmission's primary drive was to be chain-driven, but this gear-drive setup is preferable, because it should prove more reliable over the life of the bike and is considerably quieter than chain-drive.

## On Any Sunday . . .

The introduction of Senior Project Engineer John Garms to the Victory project may be the best example of how tight the staffing and lead time were for this motorcycle. Garms arrived in Osceola on a Sunday—and started work that very day.

There was no "enjoy some cheese and a Packers game on TV, and we'll see you Monday." It was more like, "This tranny needs work. Can you come in today?"

Preliminary work on the V92C's five-speed gearbox had been done months earlier by non-Victory engineers in Polaris' Roseau facility. By the time Garms came on board in September 1996, the transmission was out of sync with the rest of the bike's development. Major reworking was required.

"We have changed everything except the number of teeth and the center-to-center distance," Garms said. "Everything else has changed, and there's in the neighborhood of 135 parts through the powertrain."

In the original design, durability of some drivetrain components was questionable, as was their ability to fit together. On paper, individually, the parts looked fine, but when it came time for them to work together, well, no way.

*The oil-cooling system was given special attention to ensure that the Victory would cool properly. The larger cooler tested extremely well, keeping the bike running at acceptable temperatures even while toting the sidecar test rig in 100-degree heat.*

Garms was a good man to tackle the job, with more than two decades of engine testing and development under his belt, including a stint at Harley-Davidson, where he was part of the team that developed the Evolution engine. Before joining Victory, Garms worked for Cummins Diesel, where engines weren't measured in cc's but liters, as in the 45-liter V-12 he worked on before heading to Osceola.

Now that it's been thoroughly sorted out and brought in step with the rest of the evolving bike, the Victory powertrain consists of a gear-driven primary drive with a torque compensator; a large-diameter, multi-plate wet clutch; a five-speed gearbox with what could be considered oversized gears; and a belt-driven final drive.

The gears, clutch, and some other powertrain components are stout, probably beefier than necessary. That's for durability and reliability but also because of the late restart on transmission development and the tight production schedule. Given the time, the team might make the powertrain lighter and more compact in future iterations. Garms estimated that some parts, such as gears, are 20 to 25 percent oversized, but he also noted that the team hadn't experienced a single gear train failure with the production-ready setup.

"Our drivetrain's even bigger than Harley-Davidson's, but we're going to be pulling twice the horsepower," Garms said. "At the horsepower level we're at, we have a

*Mounted between the crankshaft and transmission, the Victory's balance shaft allows the engine to vibrate just a bit, even though it could have been designed to eliminate nearly all vibration. Motorcycles need to have personality; a little rumble here and tingle there lets you know that the machine underneath you is alive and kicking.*

*The short piston used in conjunction with short rods to shorten the top end is visible in this cutaway engine displayed at dealer shows in the fall of 1997. The single overhead cam was selected to reduce the height of the engine. Dual overhead cams would have made the engine much higher. Michael Dapper*

robust design to handle the power. This is the flagship, the first vehicle, and it's felt that what we have today should handle all the horsepower requirements that are going to be asked of it. It fits the envelope, too—that 'shoe box' on the back of the engine."

The torque compensator smoothes out some of the engine's impulses that are transmitted back to the powertrain and lessens gear train noise. In layman's terms, here's how the compensator operates: When the pistons go through their power strokes and the fuel/air mixtures are ignited, there are two firing impulses fairly close together. The torque compensator takes the edge off those impulses, storing about 15 percent of each impulse in a spring-equipped mechanism, then returning the energy to the crankshaft as it rotates with the pistons' stroking.

"Our primary goals are to take this harshness off the gear train and lower the gear noise," Garms said.

# 5

# SLOWING DOWN BEFORE TAKING OFF
## Final Developments Before Starting Production

Ask 10 motorsports enthusiasts to define performance, and you'll probably hear "it's power and speed" from six of them. A couple more might mention handling as part of performance, but only the most thorough respondent will mention braking as a facet of performance.

There's so much emphasis on "go" power—"How big's the engine?" "How quick is it from 0 to 60?" "How fast will it go?"—that slowing a bike down is an afterthought to many a consumer.

To members of the Victory team, however, effective braking was a primary concern. They realized that with the V92C's impressive power

*The Victory team cast off the veil of secrecy surrounding its new machine on February 19, 1997, when a press release announced that Polaris would be entering the motorcycle market. Rumors had run rampant since the previous fall, but the release was the first official acknowledgment of the bike's existence.*

and its responsive, confidence-inspiring handling, riders are going to push this bike to feel how well a cruiser can perform; riders are going to wring it out in curves and corners, not idle through them in an upright position.

The Victory team set out to develop braking that replicates the incredible braking of high-performance sport bikes, rather than the softer, slower braking more commonly found on cruisers.

Braking was an aspect of performance subjectively evaluated in staffers' benchmarking of competitive motorcycles, so they had goals and knew which setups provided the feel and stopping power they desired. Then they faced the challenge of measuring or judging whether their brakes achieved those goals.

As with so many other aspects of the project, the team came up with a creative approach with which to tackle the challenge and, eventually, achieved success.

On June 26, 1997, the Victory was rolled out to the press at Planet Hollywood in the Mall of America in Bloomington, Minnesota. Flash bulbs popped, Al Unser Jr. rode a preproduction bike into the restaurant, and Victory team members fielded questions about the new bike.

## A New Look at Braking

When developing an engine, it's entirely possible, even easy, to measure whether you've achieved your goals. If dyno and road testing show you've got the horsepower and true, usable power you sought, you're good to go.

But how do you measure or quantify something that's subjective, such as the way a bike's brake should feel? That was a challenge undertaken by Test Engineer Robin Tuluie. As mentioned, the team's challenge was to accurately determine whether it had instilled desired braking traits and performance in their brake system.

Tuluie developed a way to apply instrumentation to a braking system so team members could quantify braking; they could apply numbers—figures they would compare and analyze—to braking feel and effectiveness.

"We liked using data acquisition because of riders' subjectivity," he said. "You design a [braking] system to fulfill the requirements, then test it again to see if it's really what you want."

After considering brake components from six suppliers, the Victory team tested systems from a couple of companies and chose to use Brembo hardware. The team assembled a brake system using a combination of Brembo components that gave it the numbers—and feel—it wanted. Brembo technicians worked with the Victory team, and a Brembo test rider was particularly helpful in assisting the team's pursuit of the desired feel and responsiveness.

"We specified the system [to Brembo], and as much as possible, we tried to use off-the-shelf parts," Tuluie said. "Brembo doesn't make a master cylinder in the size we deemed best for the front brake, however, so we made up our own."

The braking feel the Victory team desired consisted of "linear" braking in front and digressive braking in the rear.

"For the front brake, we want it predictable, and if you pull it twice as hard, you want it to brake twice as hard," Tuluie said. "But you can lock up a rear brake, so you want to make a brake that stops the bike but doesn't

*Led by Geoff Burgess (in light shirt, directly behind the bike), this group of people gave their all to the design and development of the V92C. At the time this photo was taken January 25, 1998, the team focused on nailing down the final details before production started.*

lock up; as you push harder on it, you don't want it to decelerate quite as hard. For us, this was done by adjusting a certain lever geometry in the rear brake."

In the early stages of the Victory project, significant braking evaluation and testing was done on Francis the Mule in Tennessee. ("We eventually shut the Tennessee testing site down because people found out we were there," said Matt Parks. "At first it was great. It was a tiny town, but then people found out, and we got to be big fish in a little pond. We'd come out and people would be waiting to see the bike.")

In production form, the front brakes consist of a 300-mm floating rotor with a four-piston caliper. That's twice the pistons of the rear brake, which also uses a 300-mm floating rotor with a dual-piston caliper.

The V92C uses Dunlop tires mounted on 16-inch, cast, custom-made aluminum wheels. The Victory script logo is printed on one of the five spokes of each wheel (on both sides of each wheel). The logo is positioned near the rim so it is visible just beyond the brake rotor on the front right and rear left sides of the bike.

*The Victory made an August 1997 appearance among the faithful at the rally in Sturgis, South Dakota. The Victory's clean look—hidden plug wires, air cleaner, and shocks—had many Sturgis attendees asking if it was just a mock-up. To drive home the fact that the bike was a runner, a couple of Victory staffers rolled the bikes into the street, fired them up, and dished up a couple of smoky burnouts at the end of the day. Victory*

## A Style All Its Own

The old saying is that you shouldn't trust a motorcycle you can't see through. If that's the case, riders can put all their faith in the V92C, whose styling is clean, sharp, and free of fake covers and excessive trim.

The V92C was styled to have a distinctive, original look yet evoke the image of traditional American-made cruisers. It succeeds by showing off what's real about a cruiser: a big V-twin, gleaming pipes, a big gas tank, flowing fenders, stout front suspension, and wide handlebars.

Designer Dave Otto and General Manager Matt Parks focused on keeping the look clean, rather than loaded up with covers, badges, and trim. The idea was to make the bike appealing

*This brochure featuring a very early CV bike was the first piece of promotional literature created for the bike. Note the tiny oil cooler and two bolts holding the fender to the rear subframe. The oil cooler would be enlarged significantly on production units, and the subframe would be lengthened, adding a third bolt to the rear fender. Victory*

*During the week of the press introduction at Planet Hollywood, select journalists were invited to visit the Osceola, Wisconsin, facility. A few were allowed to take the company's only prototype for test rides. Mark Tuttle Jr. of* Rider *magazine, shown riding the bike through the Osceola countryside, was told that if he dropped the bike, "You won't even hear the rifle shot." Wayne Davis*

and let its performance do the talking. (On the street, it's likely no two V92Cs will look the same, as owners will put their own customizing signatures on the bikes.)

Working from direction offered primarily by Parks, the Brooks Stevens design firm in Milwaukee, Wisconsin, produced the original concept drawings of the bike. The Victory team selected elements of those drawings they liked, the concepts were refined, and the bike's look evolved. Throughout the project, Victory staffers offered input on assorted design and styling touches. Since virtually every member of the team is an avid and experienced motorcyclist, Parks took their input—likes, dislikes, and

*Once the team had the first preproduction bikes built, the daunting task of testing a brand-new design began in earnest. The suspension needed to tested and tuned, EPA standards had to be met, instruments calibrated, long-term reliability checked, and every little quirk caught and corrected.*

*Victory test riders recorded fuel used, mileage, and any problems on a strip of duct tape on the tank. Development technician Scott Dieltz records fuel consumption in a CV bike after a gas stop during testing on November 10, 1997.*

suggestions—to heart and has said that "everybody in the group has his signature on that bike somewhere."

One Dave Otto touch: The headlight housing design is echoed in the design of the turn indicator housings, front and rear. Atop the headlight is the V92C's extensive instrumentation: a speedometer with a small tachometer at its base and a small liquid-crystal display (LCD) panel that offers a collection of data (odometer, trip meter, clock, alternator, oil temp and fuel gauge.) A rider can scroll through this data using handlebar-mounted buttons and can reset various functions using those buttons. The speedometer face also has several back-lit symbols (high-beam, turn-signal, low-oil, low-gas, and low-generator indicators).

The colors available for the first-year V92C paint are Antares Red and KYSO (Knock

*Testing in inclement weather was part of the process, although it was not always intentional. As his fellow test riders try to figure out how to get off of the mountains before the rain turns to snow, Scott Dieltz looks in vain for a break in the sky. Things would get worse before they got better; heavy fog, steady rain, freezing temperatures, and rock slides would have the Victory test riders dodging boulders in near-zero visibility before the day was done.*

Your Socks Off) Blue. (Antares is an ancient, giant red star, the brightest in the constellation Scorpio.) The Victory script logo appears in several places (wheel spokes, case covers, handlebar clamp), but the full-color Victory graphic only appears on the gas tank badge.

## Making Short Work of Long-Term Testing

Several test methods were used to evaluate the V92C's durability, including extended test rides between Osceola and the team's western test site. There were also engine durability tests consisting of 24-hour dyno tests at the Polaris facility in Roseau and grueling sessions on special road-wear simulators.

Preproduction bikes underwent testing on simulators that recreated the rigors of road travel—in a hurry. Tuluie said a Victory test bike was mounted on the hydraulic ramps of an MTS Systems simulator, and in just 10 days it endured the rigors of 30,000 miles of travel.

"The only thing that damages the chassis is a bump—a smooth road causes no damage—so the system cuts out all sections of smooth road [from its prerecorded road input data]," Tuluie said. "You end up with an accelerated durability

*The Victory engine is built at the Osceola, Wisconsin, facility. This preproduction engine is being hand-assembled by Group Leader Mike Benoy. Blueprints like the one on the wall, computer drawings, and parts lists were used to assemble the preproduction engines. Early assemblies were test beds themselves, as assembly problems were discovered and eliminated.*

*The carbon steel frames are welded together at this robotic welding station in Spirit Lake, Iowa.* Michael Dapper

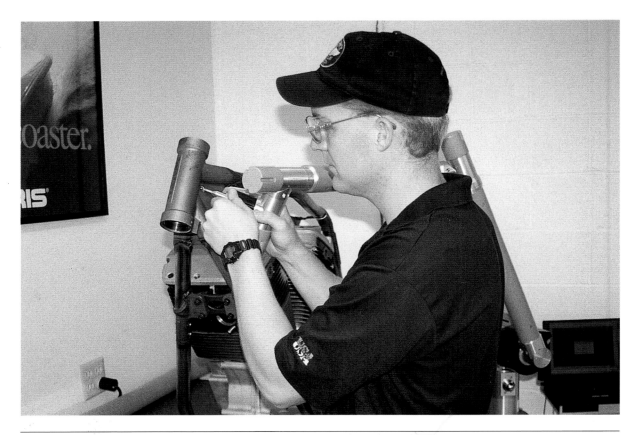

Another part of shaking down the manufacturing process was to evaluate early examples to be sure they were coming out within specifications. This preproduction frame is being measured by a test technician. Michael Dapper

test that's approximately 20 times as short as it would take to perform this test on the road. The bike hits all the bumps of a 2-hour ride in about 10 minutes."

After a Victory test bike withstood 30,000 miles worth of abuse on the simulator, its failures were evaluated, and there was good news and bad news. It was bad that the team discovered *any* failures, but they were the same problems as those revealed from road testing, giving the team confidence in both test methods (real riding and the simulator). Parts were redesigned, and the new parts were installed on a test bike that went through a test simulating

more than 60,000 miles of bad roads.

"With the simulator, you find out everything, from whether your mirrors are rattling to how good your seat is," said Parks. "The only thing it doesn't have is engine vibration, and the thought is that if anything fails *without* engine vibration, it will certainly fail *with* engine vibration."

In another version of accelerated durability testing, bikes were driven on a proving ground test track so rough that 1 mile on the track is the equivalent of 5 miles of road travel. The bikes were ridden hard on the track, and they endured tremendous jarring, bumps, and vibrations.

## A Well-Traveled Bike

The Victory motorcycle project has touched almost as many states as a vintage travel trailer. The go-ahead for the motorcycle project came from Polaris' corporate headquarters in Minneapolis, and initial engineering was done in Roseau before the Victory team moved to its engineering facility in Osceola, Wisconsin. (Engines are assembled at Osceola, and the complete motorcycle is assembled at Polaris' Spirit Lake, Iowa plant.)

Developmental testing has been done in several states, including Minnesota and Wisconsin, of course, as well as Tennessee, where some early work was done, primarily with Francis the Mule, and Arizona, where the most significant benchmarking rides took place.

In Colorado, the electronic fuel injection (EFI) system was calibrated for various altitudes, and the team has long had a test facility in the south that is blessed by a desert climate for year-round testing. It also gives staffers quick access to mountain elevations and wide-open desert roads for, among other things, heat, fuel range, speed, and durability testing. Test bikes have also been ridden, not trucked, between Wisconsin and California—and to points in between.

*Final assembly takes place on a production line at the Spirit Lake, Iowa, plant. The engine is lifted and fastened to the cradle, and the rest of the bike is bolted up. This is one of the first few bikes to be built on the line, at a time when only one cradle was available. These final preproduction units were known as P bikes.*

*This side view of an early Victory production bike was taken in the summer of 1997. Although this bike is quite complete, the Victory received a host of subtle but significant changes before being released to the public. Wayne Davis*

## First Impressions

No matter how good a motorcycle the Victory team developed, it wouldn't matter without an effective promotional effort. Judging by preproduction interest in the bike as this book went to press, the effort has been a success, and demand for Victory motorcycles will likely outstrip supply for a couple years—at least.

The first official word of the Victory project's existence came when Polaris announced on February 19, 1997, that it was entering the motorcycle business. The announcement came in a press release distributed by the company's public relations agency, Shandwick USA. The release was accompanied by a teasing color photo of the Victory logo but not the motorcycle.

The bike was first viewed publicly at the Planet Hollywood restaurant at the Mall of America in Bloomington, Minnesota, on June 26, 1997. Indy car racer Al Unser Jr. rode the bike into the packed restaurant to give the gathered media, Polaris staffers, and invited guests their first look—and listen.

The following day, editors from several motorcycle magazines met the Victory staff in Osceola to learn more about the bike. A select few took it for a first-impression ride. The result was universally positive reviews in the motorcycle press. It has also received coverage in newspapers such as the *Wall Street Journal*, *New York Times*, and *USA Today*, and Matt Parks has appeared on television networks such as CNN and CNBC.

A couple of V92Cs were on display at the annual Sturgis rally in August 1997, and they were running models of near-production quality,

not just show bikes. They laid down some rubber on Sturgis' Main Street during the week on trips between downtown and the team's rented home.

A Victory web site on the Internet was launched in the summer of 1997, and the first group of U.S. Victory dealers was announced in mid-November of that year. An advertising campaign, posters, brochures, and related marketing materials were produced by Stahl & Associates, the ad agency run by Jerry Stahl, who had played an integral role early in the Victory project when motorcycle market research was conducted.

Show bikes drew crowds at motorcycle shows throughout the fall of 1997 and the winter that followed, and the first Victory dealer convention, complete with dealer demo rides, was held in January 1998 in Palm Springs, California.

The public got its first chance to ride the new motorcycle on demo rides at Daytona Bike Week in March 1998, and production models rolled out of the Spirit Lake production plant just before this book was published.

## A Long and Rewarding Journey

On the sunny morning in June 1997 when the V92C was shown publicly for the first time, members of the Victory team were all smiles. Finally, their big day had come.

For parts of the previous three years, they had invested what seemed like countless hours in dyno cells, on the seats of test bikes, staring at design station monitors, in meeting rooms, at drafting tables, and in hotel rooms far from home.

Most of them had slept only a handful of hours in the weeks before the all-important public introduction, and they knew that the next day they would be back at work, refining designs, seeking answers, spinning wrenches, and crunching numbers.

But those pressing matters could wait 24 hours because, for a glorious day in the midst of one of the busiest years of their collective lives, they paused to bask in the raucous applause that ushered their two-wheeled baby to the front of the room at Planet Hollywood. At once exhausted, relieved, and giddy, some of them cried. Others lit cigars—Victory cigars, of course—and all accepted hugs and handshakes of congratulations.

As they posed with the bike for a team photo outside the restaurant, it struck some of them as ridiculous, impossible, and certainly amazing that virtually everyone who had played significant roles in the development of the V92C could fit in one group shot. Large teams of consultants, engineers, and managers weren't absent. No, all hands were there, and it was a remarkably few hands that had created this historic new American-made cruiser in just three years after the company's directors approved the project.

Following the introduction, the team faced yet another massive set of challenges, namely to put finishing touches on the bike and then mass-produce it to exacting standards. Ah, well, if there weren't a heavy mantle of pressure and expectations on their shoulders, they probably wouldn't know how to act.

Their rewards included hearing the cheers at Planet Hollywood and getting the thumbs-up from riders at Sturgis, Daytona, and shows across the country. Fortunate riders will get their rewards once they take delivery of the highly collectible 1998 models. Each of the first-year U.S. Victory dealers was expected to receive approximately 10 bikes. Their happy customers will apply their customizing touches to the bikes, pull on the denim, leather, and black T-shirts, and ride a piece of rolling history down the open road—the road to Victory.

# SPECIFICATIONS

| | |
|---|---|
| Model name | V92C |
| Length | 94 inches |
| Wheelbase | 63.31 inches |
| Seat height | 28 inches |
| Ground clearance | 5.51 inches |
| Dry weight | 637 pounds |
| | |
| Engine type | Air/oil-cooled 50-degree V-twin, 4-stroke |
| Bore x stroke | 97x102-mm |
| Displacement | 1,507-cc (91.92 cubic inches) |
| Valvetrain | Single overhead cam; self-adjusting cam chains; 4 -valves per cylinder; hydraulic lifters |
| Lubrication | Dry sump |
| Oil capacity | 6 quarts |
| Fuel system | Electronic Fuel Injection with 44-mm throttle bores |
| Fuel capacity | 5 U.S. gallons |
| Exhaust | Staggered dual exhaust |
| | |
| Primary drive | Gear drive with torque compensator |
| Clutch | Wet, multi-plate |
| Transmission | 5-speed |
| Final drive | Belt-drive |
| | |
| Front suspension | 45-mm Marzocchi fork tubes; 5.12 inches of travel |
| Rear suspension | Triangulated swing arm, single Fox shock with spring preload adjustability, 4 inches of travel |
| Front brakes | 300-mm floating rotor with four-piston caliper |
| Rear brakes | 300-mm floating rotor with two-piston caliper |
| Front wheel | 16.0x3.0-inch, five-spoke cast-aluminum wheels |
| Rear wheel | 16.0x3.5-inch, five-spoke cast-aluminum wheels |
| Front tire | 16-inch Dunlop Elite 2 MT90 |
| Rear tire | 160/80 Dunlop Elite 2 MT90 |
| Frame | Tubular steel with aluminum subframe; uses the engine as a stressed member |
| | |
| Instrumentation | Electronic speedometer and tachometer with odometer, resettable tripmeter, fuel gauge,high-beam indicator, oil light, turn signal indicators, low-fuel light, low-voltage light and clock |
| | |
| Lights | Twin-beam headlight, turn signals (front and rear), tail/brake light |
| Paint colors | Antares Red/black and KYSO Blue/black |
| | |
| Manufacturer | Victory Motorcycle Division, Polaris Industries Inc., 1225 Hwy. 169 N., Minneapolis, MN 55441 |
| Internet web site | www.victory-usa.com |

# INDEX